Getting Skills Right

Incentives for SMEs to Invest in Skills

LESSONS FROM EUROPEAN GOOD PRACTICES

This work is published under the responsibility of the Secretary-General of the OECD. The opinions expressed and arguments employed herein do not necessarily reflect the official views of the Members of the OECD.

The report was co-funded by the European Union via the Structural Reform Support Programme (REFORM/IM2020/004).

This publication was produced with the financial assistance of the European Union. The views expressed herein can in no way be taken to reflect the official opinion of the European Union.

This document, as well as any data and map included herein, are without prejudice to the status of or sovereignty over any territory, to the delimitation of international frontiers and boundaries and to the name of any territory, city or area.

Please cite this publication as:
OECD (2021), *Incentives for SMEs to Invest in Skills: Lessons from European Good Practices*, Getting Skills Right, OECD Publishing, Paris, *https://doi.org/10.1787/1eb16dc7-en*.

ISBN 978-92-64-89355-9 (print)
ISBN 978-92-64-34748-9 (pdf)

Getting Skills Right
ISSN 2520-6117 (print)
ISSN 2520-6125 (online)

Photo credits: Cover Cell phone: © Creative Commons/Alfredo Hernandez; clock: © Creative Commons/Hakan Yalcin; cloud upload: © Creative Commons/Warsla; join: © Creative Commons/Tom Ingebretsen; doctor: © Creative Commons/Joseph Wilson; chef: © Creative Commons/Alfonso Melolontha, and Gearings image © OECD, designed by Christophe Brilhault.

Corrigenda to publications may be found on line at: *www.oecd.org/about/publishing/corrigenda.htm*.

Foreword

Employers across the world are adjusting production processes as a consequence of the COVID-19 shock and the pressure of structural transformations such technological transitions, demographic changes or globalisation. In many instances, these transformations require employers to update the skills of their workforce via new hires or worker training. This challenging process is hampered by a range of market failures, in particular for micro, small and medium-sized enterprises (SMEs), which results in socially sub-optimal investment in skills and justifies governments' intervention. Based on the analysis of the existing policy landscape and economic literature, this report identifies practices that were successful in supporting SMEs' investment in skills in different countries of the European Union. It describes the design and rationale of these instruments, while providing a critical assessment over their advantages and limitations.

The report is structured around four chapters. Chapter 1 presents the economic rationale and scope for policy intervention to promote training by employers and SMEs in particular. The remainder of the report describes the most common tools that policy makers can use to support investment in skills by SMEs in skills. Some policies reduce the direct or indirect cost of reskilling (Chapter 2), while others develop the skills of managers and entrepreneurs, their awareness of the firm's reskilling needs, and their capacity to hire and train workers (Chapter 3). Chapter 4 looks at policies that leverage the firm's relationships with the training ecosystem, including other firms, education institutions and the public sector, to shape the firm's investment in skills. Chapter 5 concludes and identifies a number of features in common across the identified good practices.

This report was prepared by Luca Marcolin from the Directorate for Employment, Labour and Social Affairs, with contributions from Michela Meghnagi and Maryam Shater, and under the supervision of Glenda Quintini (Skills team manager) and Mark Keese (Head of the Skills and Employability Division). Useful comments were provided by Simone Marino and Claudia Piferi (DG REFORM, European Commission), and Mattia Corbetta and Alessandra Proto (OECD). This report is published under the responsibility of the Secretary General of the OECD, with the financial assistance of the European Union via the Structural Reform Support Programme. The views expressed in this report should not be taken to reflect the official position of OECD member countries nor the official position of the European Union.

Table of contents

FIGURES

Executive summary

Small and medium-sized enterprises (SMEs) constitute a large part of the economy in all OECD countries. To remain competitive and adaptable to the challenges brought about by globalisation, technological progress, demographic and climate change, SMEs must maintain and expand their access to skills and talent.

Despite this imperative, SMEs often experience severe shortages of skills and in particular digital talent. They are less successful in attracting and retaining skilled workers; they face higher direct and indirect costs of training the workforce; and they tend to lack information on the state of the labour market and the available training opportunities and support mechanisms. Public intervention is therefore needed to facilitate training in SMEs and greater access to the existing talent pool, above and beyond the support given to large firms.

Drawing from national examples across Europe, this report identifies policies and programmes that have proved successful in supporting SMEs' investment in skills, highlighting implementation features, governance structure, and other success factors. The overview table at the end of this section summarises the measures identified as good practices, and classifies them into four main groups, depending on the barrier they help overcome, and the financial or non-financial nature of the initiative.

Financial incentives are aimed at lowering the costs of training employees and hiring talent. Among the financial incentives that governments can mobilise, **subsidies and vouchers** are the most used and suitable instrument to target SMEs. Schemes can target small employers exclusively or provide them with more comprehensive or greater support or simplified procedures. Subsidies are flexible, and can easily be tailored to respond to specific needs and target groups, but should be designed to minimise the administrative burden for employers. Vouchers, in particular, are scalable and transferrable.

Pay-back clauses, which make employees liable for some or all of the costs of their training if they leave their employer within some stipulated period, are non-financial measures that strengthen firms' incentives to offer train by decreasing the risk associated with *poaching*. To be effective, they need to strike a good balance between the employee's right to move across jobs, and the employer's need to recover the training expenses incurred. They must include clauses in case the training participant is insolvent, and spell out in detail the content of the training and the provisions for extra-judicial settlement.

Learning on the job is the most common form of training but it is mostly not formally recognised. Encouraging its recognition not only helps employers and workers to reap its benefits but also allows policy makers to support it financially. **Job rotation schemes**, albeit relatively rare in micro and small-sized firms, can also support the informal sharing of knowledge among peers of different units or functions, while benefiting the firm as a whole.

Skill Assessment and Anticipation (SAA) services are used to assess the firm's skills gaps relative to current and future needs. They can be offered by operators such as Public Employment Services, learning networks or consultants. They can also be developed in-house by SMEs with public support. **Diagnostic tools** for SAA are affordable and can be implemented through simple online employee surveys. The promotion of modern HR systems, **High Performance Working Practices** and other forms of workplace innovation usually combine co-funding or sharing of costs to implement workplace interventions with other services, including guidance and knowledge and best practice dissemination.

The attitude of managers and entrepreneurs towards learning in the firm is also crucial in the firm's investment in skills. Investing in the competences of managers and entrepreneurs, and their understanding of human capital as a productive investment, can therefore enhance SMEs' growth and survival. **Coaching, mentoring and peer learning** among managers promote knowledge sharing and transfer, and build on concrete practices from successful entrepreneurs. Firms, however, also require operational support when it comes to implementing solutions. Measures that combine peer learning and individual support services, for example through subsidised consulting or coaching services, seem to be best placed to support investment in the key competences for the digital transformation.

Co-operation among companies and between companies and other stakeholders allows for the pooling of resources, economies of scale, and the building of a critical mass in the demand for training that decreases the per-worker cost of training. **Learning and training networks** often provide companies with subsidies for the development of the networks, subsidies for the training activities themselves, guidance on financial incentives available to cover the costs of training, or direct expertise through public skills assessments.

Similarly, the promotion and strengthening of skills ecosystems and of partnerships between companies, e.g. via **competence centres,** can be successful in promoting digitalisation and knowledge transfers to SMEs. The centres are one of several effective measures facilitating the creation of skills ecosystems.

While available, these policy instruments are not all equivalent in their take-up by SMEs, nor in their ability to successfully increase investment in skills in SMEs. Existing monitoring and evaluation data for these policies, albeit not frequently available, suggest that many of the described policies reach an overall limited share of the potential SMEs. If this is the result of a complex set of economic and institutional factors that falls outside the scope of this report, the joint analysis of good practices allows identifying a number of common elements of policy design, which can increase the take-up and effectiveness of such policies.

- Participation and satisfaction about reskilling initiatives are higher when the administrative burden is low, and when there is certainty of funding.
- For financial instruments, the generosity of the funding received is an incentive to participation, but private-public co-funding or cost-sharing models remain the most effective and most common.
- Larger investments in skills can be obtained by factoring-in the indirect costs of training, and informal learning activities besides formal and non-formal ones.
- Many programmes combine financial and non-financial support, as this can increase the uptake and raise the return on the financial support. Non-financial tools help firms that do not recognise the need to invest or are uncertain about how to set up the investment.
- Programmes should respond to specific needs of individual companies. Measures that include good-practices and knowledge sharing are therefore most suitable for SMEs.
- Policies should allow for flexible delivery, especially for the training of managers, which can be achieved with modular courses and online training.
- Open and proactive communication between companies and the agencies managing training support measures increases the take up of these measures by SMEs. Indeed providing accurate but accessible information on the availability and functioning of the policy instrument is a key component of the policy's success.
- Strategies to increase participation in networks with other companies or other stakeholders include awareness raising activities, early and personal contact with companies, and peer learning activities for managers and entrepreneurs.

Overview of identified measures

Objective	Type of measures	Country good practices
Lowering the cost of reskilling: Financial measures		
Lowering direct and indirect costs of reskilling	Subsidies, e.g. Vouchers for training, Vouchers for consulting services, Grants	Qualification-Opportunities -Law (Qualifizierungschancengesetz) – DEU MKB! Dee subsidy – NLD Go Inno / Go Digital vouchers – DEU
	Subsidised schemes and support services for training	Joint Purchase Training system (Yhteishankintakoulutus / Gemensam anskaffning av utbildning) – FIN
	Others: Tax incentives, Levy schemes	
Lowering the cost of reskilling: Non-financial measures		
Lowering indirect costs	Job Rotation schemes	Job rotation scheme (Jobrotationsordningen) – DNK
Expanding the coverage scope of costs of public funding to other reskilling initiatives	Inclusion of informal training in subsidised training	Learning at the workplace (AFEST) – FRA
Mitigating poaching risks	Payback clauses	Payback clause (Scholingsbeding) – NLD
Support measures to build SMEs' capacity and learning culture		
Improving information on skill needs (Matching; Skill Assessment and Anticipation) Promoting HR capacity, workplace innovation Strengthening managerial skills	Diagnostic tools for skills anticipation and analysis and workforce innovation	Regional Skill Fora – IRL Advance Management of Skills (Gestion prévisionnelle des emplois et des compétences – GPEC) – FRA Workplace Innovation Tool – IRL Smart Diag' Tool – FRA
	HR support services and counselling, consulting	Joint Purchase Training system (Yhteishankintakoulutus/ Gemensam anskaffning av utbildning) – FIN Enterprise Value: the People (UnternehmensWert: Mensch – uMV) – DEU Innova South – GRC, ITA Telework Action Plan – BEL
	Peer-learning	Be the Business – GBR EI Mentor Network – IRL Scale-up Denmark – DNK
	Coaching and mentoring for managers and entrepreneurs	Kickstart Digitalisation (Kickstart Digitalisering) – SWE Turin Chamber of Commerce – ITA EI Mentor Network – IRL Scale-up Denmark – DNK
	Competence centres	Competence Centre on securing skilled labour (KOFA) – DEU
Support measures to promote co-operation among companies and with the public/education sector		
Creating economies of scale, pooling of information and resources Promoting collaboration among firms Promoting collaboration in the ecosystem	Learning networks	Joint Purchase Training system (Yhteishankintakoulutus/ Gemensam anskaffning av utbildning) – FIN Impulse Training Networks (Implus-Qualifizierungs-Verbund) – AUT Skillsnet Training Networks Programme – IRL
	Industry-science co-operation	Mittelstand 4.0-Kompetenzzentren – DEU Competence Centres for Excellent Technologies (COMET) – AUT Katapult – NLD

1 Investment in Skills in SMEs

SMEs constitute a large part of the economy and play a key role in ensuring that our economies and societies can adapt to today's major transformations – globalisation, technological progress, demographic change and environmental change. In order to remain competitive and in the face of these challenges, SMEs need to secure access to skills and talent by attracting and retaining skilled workers, as well as up-skilling or reskilling their workforce.

Skilled workers are a key component of firms' competiveness in a knowledge-based economy, but SMEs are often less successful in hiring and retaining skilled workers than larger firms, especially workers with management, communication or problem-solving skills, which are crucial for innovation. Their employees are also less likely on average to participate in formal and non-formal job-related learning. (OECD, 2019[1]; OECD, 2019[2]). For instance, almost all (91%) large firms in the EU27+United Kingdom provided at least one continuing vocational training (CVT) course to their workers in 2015, as opposed to 77% of medium and 57% of small firms (Figure 1.1, Panel A). These shares differ across countries, with particularly low shares of firms engaging in training in Greece, Hungary, Latvia and Poland, but in all countries there is a considerable gap between larger and smaller companies. Even where smaller companies do offer training, the number of hours of training per worker is generally smaller than in larger firms offering training. Notable exceptions are Ireland and the United Kingdom, where small firms invest longer hours per worker in CVT courses than medium-sized and large firms, a fact that deserves further consideration in the future.[1] The same gap between smaller and large companies also exists for other types of learning activities beside CVT courses such as guided on-the-job training, rotation schemes, conferences and workshops, learning and quality circles.

Indeed SMEs face a number of challenges when it comes to investment in training and skill development of their staff: on average, they have less time and resources to devote to training, they have less understanding of what training systems can do to address their workplace needs, and they have more limited access to credit (OECD, 2017[3]; OECD, 2019[2]). SMEs tend to lack information on training opportunities or support mechanisms that are available to them, as well as on the benefits of investing in training relative to the perceived risks. Generally, smaller companies tend to be more reluctant to invest in human capital they could lose (e.g. because of poaching) and face higher opportunity costs of training, especially one that happens during working hours but outside the firm's boundaries. The direct cost of training an employee may also be higher, if the firm cannot benefit of economies of scale, or if the initial cost of searching suitable opportunities can only be split over a limited number of training participants. Lastly, SMEs' are less able to identify their skills needs and attract the right talent than in larger companies (Stone, 2012[4]). They usually have less developed human resource management systems, while owners and managers do not always have the capability to identify skill requirements in relation to training needs and talent acquisition, or to design an effective strategy for skill acquisition and development.

Figure 1.1. Continuing vocational training (CVT), by firm size

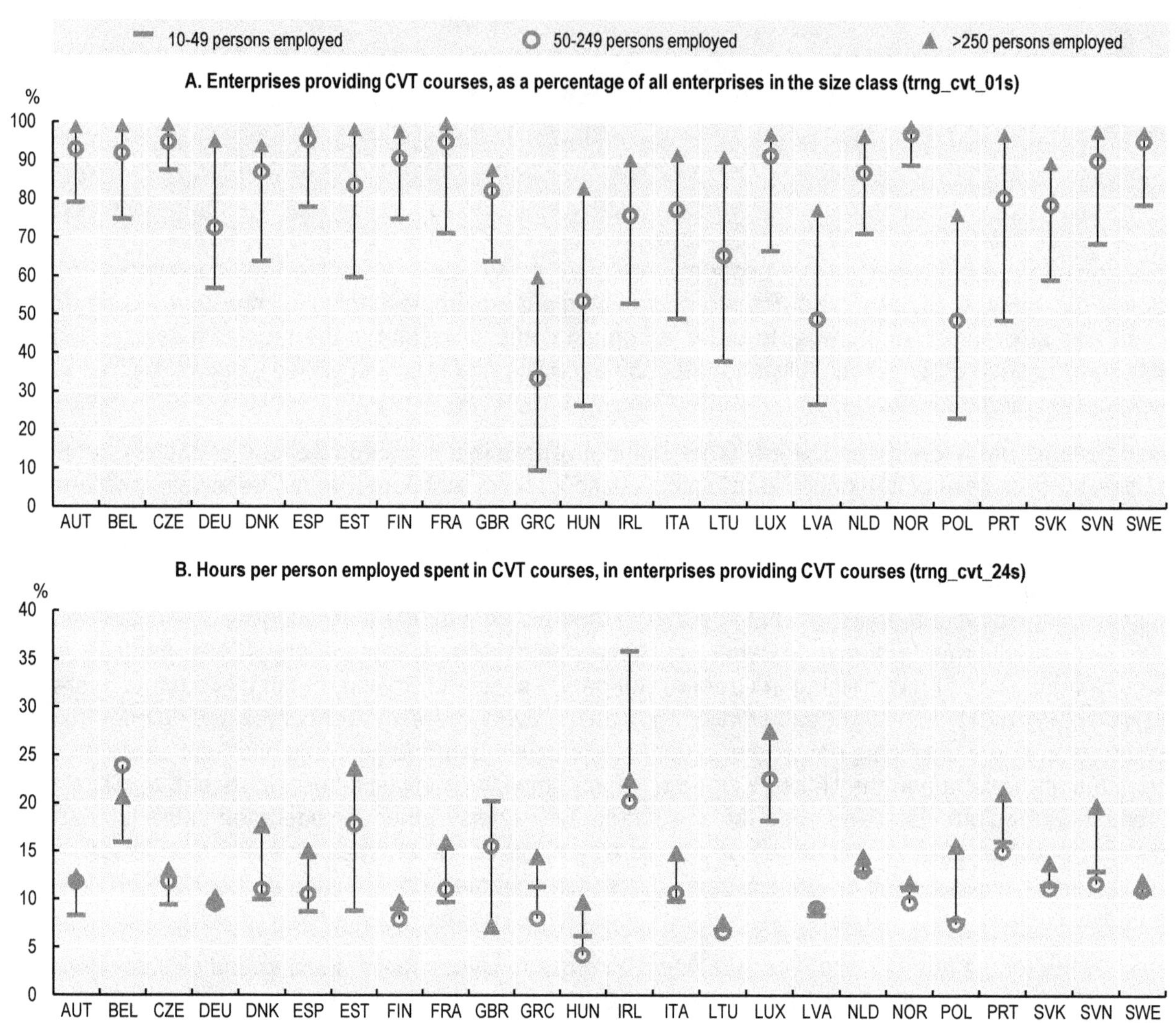

Note: The survey covers only firms with ten persons employed or more.
Source: European Continuing Vocational Training Survey (CVTS), 2015.

These challenges are further amplified in the context of technological transitions, as small businesses on average adopt new technologies at a slower pace than larger companies (OECD, 2018[5]; OECD, 2020[6]). Beyond basic levels of digitalisation, the emergence of new technologies, such as the Internet of Things, cyber security and big data creates further skills gaps, shortages and mismatches, especially for SMEs, who cannot compete with larger companies in attracting digital talent (European Commission, 2020[7]; OECD, 2021[8]). Skills shortages are registered at every level in the hierarchy of SMEs, from e-Leadership skills to ICT-professionals to users' digital skills, with SMEs running the risk of remaining excluded from significant market potential. Furthermore, surveys from multiple OECD countries, show that up to 70% of SMEs have increased the use of digital technologies during in 2020 (OECD, 2021[8]), which could worsen skill shortages.

The tendency for SMEs to underinvest in skills derives from a number of market failures, which are especially consequential for smaller firms (Stone, 2012[4]; OECD, 2020[6]). In this context, well-designed interventions by governments can engage employers in adult learning provision in a variety of ways and help address the misalignment between the supply and demand of skills. The purpose of this report, therefore, is to identify a range of public policies that can be effective in supporting and promoting investment in competences in micro, small and medium-sized enterprises. It presents a critical overview of instruments used across Europe, and highlights their implementation features, governance structure and success factors. In particular, the report focuses on measures that provide good examples in incentivising SMEs to invest in training their workforce, hiring skilled employees or assessing their needs.

Overall, the landscape of public policies for investments in skills is varied, with a constellation of measures at the national and regional levels, which affect both supply of, and demand for, skills and training. This report will focus on measures that target investment in skills in SMEs specifically or that benefit SMEs in particular, such as simplified procedures or greater support. It does not provide, therefore, a full review of the effectiveness of the overall adult learning system as in e.g. OECD (2019[2]; 2020[9]), despite the fact that this certainly has some bearing on SMEs' ability to find suitable human capital. Similarly, the report is not concerned with measures that target the supply of skills with the aim of making it more responsive to the needs of SMEs, such as apprenticeship systems (OECD/ILO, 2017[10]), individual learning accounts (OECD, 2019[11]), or career guidance services (OECD, 2021[12]).

Given this approach and scope, the present report is the first systematic review of international reskilling successful practices for SMEs since Stone (2012[4]), on which it expands with more recent policy examples, a broader typology of instruments, and greater focus on the design of each policy. Other recent OECD analyses have also reviewed successful reskilling practices but with a selected focus on some regions (OECD, 2013[13]), financial instruments (OECD, 2017[3]), university-industry linkages (OECD, 2018[14]) or workplace innovation practices (OECD, 2020[15]).

1.1. The structure of the report

Drawing on a range of national examples, the present report identifies policies and programmes that have proved successful in supporting SMEs' investment in skills. These initiatives are classified according to the barrier the SME faces in investing in skills: (i) cost, i.e. the direct costs of training or hiring and retaining workers with the required skills, as well as the opportunity cost of such activities; (ii) informational barriers, including the limited skills of managers and entrepreneurs; and (iii) co-ordination failures between a firm and its skills and training ecosystem (other firms, universities, the public sector). However, as firms may face several co-existing barriers, so some of the reviewed policy actions can tackle more than one barrier at the same time. Another distinction can be made between initiatives that require a change in regulation or legislation (but no financial commitment), and the majority of initiatives that imply spending or direct provision of services by the public administration. Among the latter, only a fraction provides direct financial support to firms for their reskilling activity.

Chapter 2 presents measures that aim to lower cost barriers and risks that SMEs encounter when investing in human capital. The chapter focuses mainly on financial incentives, which are broadly used to support SMEs accessing training and new talent, as well as investing in digital transformation and innovation. Among financial incentives available to governments, subsidies are the most used and suitable to target SMEs. Voucher schemes are especially frequent and, when used to acquire consulting services, have proven to be a scalable and transferrable funding scheme that allows SMEs to innovate. Also covered are tax incentives, payback clauses (which mitigate the risk of poaching) and measures that promote the recovery of costs linked to informal training, a form of learning that is often used in SMEs.

Chapter 3 focuses on measures that aim to build the capacity of SMEs to invest in human capital, supporting them in developing and accessing competences, services and structures that are instrumental to this type of investment. The chapter includes measures that support SMEs assess and anticipate their skills needs, develop the right competences and structures – such as HR functions – to offer relevant and quality training, and become innovative and attractive workplaces, where skills are used effectively. As the success of this type of measures is often linked to management and leadership skills within the company, the chapter also presents measures that focus on strengthening the learning and innovation culture, through mentoring or leadership- and management-development programmes.

Chapter 4 presents measures that promote co-operation among firms and between firms and other institutions. It highlights the importance of including SMEs within learning networks, or in digital and innovation ecosystems, as this can reduce the costs of, or foster economies of scale in, firms' investment in skills. This can happen through pooling of resources among companies or in the form of knowledge transfers.

In each chapter, a number of good practices from different European countries are presented, with a focus on practices that have proven successful in advancing SMEs investment in skills. The analysis discusses implementation details and strengths and weaknesses of the measures, and takes into consideration their potential for scalability (to other companies) and transferability (to other contexts). It also highlights how many successful cases combine financial support with the provision of direct expertise or other non-financial tools, which raise the return on the investment made.

The assessment of the success of the presented policies mainly relies on the relevant literature, discussions with institutional and non-institutional stakeholders, and the analysis of the policy design itself, and considers the potential of each measure to affect the outcome of interest (investment in skills by SMEs). In most cases, indeed, the monitoring, evaluation or review of users' opinions on these measures do not exist. For the same reason, the report does not in general look at policies from the perspective of the optimal allocation of public resources, as very little evidence exists on the counterfactual outcomes in absence of these policies in order to carry out a full cost-benefit analysis of these policies.

The good practices identified in the report are mostly, albeit not solely, taken from countries that present a high participation of SME employees in training such as Denmark, Finland, the Netherlands, Norway, United Kingdom, Sweden, Ireland, and/or are front-runners in developing SME innovation and smart growth policies, such as Germany. The focus is limited to European countries, as the report was funded by the European Commission Structural Reform Support Programme.

As each policy is embedded in its country's regulatory and policy system, effectiveness can vary across countries for the same policy, depending for instance on framework conditions and skills ecosystems that characterise the national context. Furthermore, there can be complementary policies that influence the effectiveness of the measure of interest, including policies that target the supply of training, which are not discussed in detail in this report. To the extent possible, the report tries to account for these elements while describing the good practices.

In addition, the analysis acknowledges and factors in the large diversity among SMEs, in particular in the context of the digital and green transformations. SMEs include both innovative and fast-growing companies that provide or use digital solutions, and companies that face significant challenges in acquiring the skills to benefit from these technologies. The target group is thus diverse, with different stages of corporate maturity and business goals. However, it has been noted that innovation and digital strategies may have greater impact on competitiveness and productivity when focusing on SMEs that have the propensity and capacity to lead, grow, digitise and internationalise their business (European Commission, 2020[7]). These SMEs have in fact the potential to act as intermediaries between leading companies and non-tech SMEs, thus fostering the diffusion and adoption of new technologies. This report describes measures that can best support the investment in skills for these high-potential SMEs.

2 Reducing costs and risks

One of the main obstacles SMEs face to investing in human capital is a lack of financial or human resources that enable the investment. Some policies are therefore designed to facilitate access to resources and reduce the costs that employers bear to hire skilled workforce and/or train their employees. Measures of this type can target both direct and indirect costs of training, as well as mitigate risks, such as the risk of poaching (i.e. loss of employee soon after training). With this aim, financial and non-financial incentives are often used to complement each other.

Among financial incentives, direct subsidies are very common. General in nature and flexible across different training needs, they are most suited to address the very heterogeneous needs of SMEs, and they are therefore discussed extensively in this chapter. Other financial instruments include tax incentives and training levies that are often used as a way to pool resources together across companies and earmark them for training expenditure (OECD, 2017[3]), but which do not usually target SMEs in particular. Non-financial measures include job rotation schemes, which decrease the opportunity cost of training, and payback clauses, which mitigate the risk of poaching.

When it comes to small companies, schemes can be designed as: (i) separate tools, aimed to address specifically the needs of SMEs, lowering cost barriers and/or which specifically seek to support company growth through skill investments, or (ii) part of broader schemes, but applying a different degree of support or simpler, more flexible procedures depending on company size.

No matter the instrument, a certain level of consensus has been reached on principles of good practice that should guide the design and use of financial incentives for investments in skill (OECD, 2017[3]). These principles, together with enabling framework conditions, impact the effectiveness of policies' and their take up among employers, especially SMEs (see Box 2.1).

Box 2.1. Good practice in the implementation of financial incentives for investment in skills

A OECD review of available evidence has identified a set of principles that can positively influence the design and implementation of financial incentives meant to steer training and investment in skills, including:

- Minimise administrative burdens, as complicated procedures negatively affect the use of these measures;
- Design systems that are simple and easily adaptable to new and emerging skills, for example by allowing measures to be tailored at sectoral and/or regional level;
- Involve social partners;
- Complement financial incentives with support measures and other interventions that can increase their effectiveness;
- Ensure monitoring and evaluation.

In addition to these principles, effective implementation depends on a number of framework conditions, such as:

- Robust systems and tools for assessing and anticipating skills needs;
- Impartial, accessible and accurate information, advice and guidance to employers and individuals on labour market needs and learning offers;
- Strong qualification frameworks;
- High-quality and responsive education and training supply;
- Effective public employment services
- Policy co-ordination and coherence.

Source: OECD (2017[3]), *Getting Skills Right: Financial Incentives for Steering Education and Training*, https://doi.org/10.1787/9789264272415-en.

2.1. Training subsidies for SMEs

Subsidies for employers generally fall within four categories: subsidies for work-based learning, such as apprenticeships or traineeships; subsidies to hire and train the unemployed; subsidies to train existing workers; and subsidies for joint employer solutions, which provide funding conditional on collaboration between employers or use funding to set up bodies that provide services to groups of employers (OECD, 2017[3]).

Subsidies can cover direct costs of training and/or indirect costs, such as wage costs, and can apply to all categories of employees or only to specific target groups within firms, or respond to specific needs, such as steering training toward in-demand skills and address the need for skill adjustment within the market (OECD, 2017[3]).

Often, small employers can apply for training subsidies through the Public Employment Service (PES), as in the case in the many of the examples below, and often through easy or simplified procedures aimed to ease access to the measure for SMEs. When subsidies are aimed at investment in skills relating to innovation, digitalisation or related initiatives, they can be administered by public agencies or managing bodies competent in the field (e.g. under the Ministry of Economic Affairs).

The evidence suggests that training in small firms is relatively sensitive to the availability of subsidies, with an increase in participation shown when these measures are available (Stone, 2010[16]). This type of measure is particularly suitable for SMEs, as it lowers barriers to investment while being very flexible, a tool that can be modulated to target different needs and circumstances. This in turn reduces deadweight losses, i.e. the use of public funding for firms that would have invested in skills in any case (OECD, 2017[3]). However, more systematic targeting to lower deadweight costs may generate large administration costs and reduce take up, which represent the most evident shortcoming of subsidies for training (OECD, 2017[3]). In addition, subsidies seem to be most effective when implemented together with other interventions and services, which is often the case as shown below (Stone, 2010[16]).

In **Germany**, for example, all enterprises can benefit from federal subsidies to cover direct and indirect training costs under the *Qualification-Chances-Law* (Qualifizierungschancengesetz). Training costs are subsidised to varying degrees, depending on firm size, as well as type of training, characteristics of the worker to be trained, social dialogue and share of employers in need of skill adjustment. Smaller companies receive higher shares of support than larger companies and the subsidy covers both direct and indirect costs, again with differences by type of workers and companies. The law has come in to force as part of the national training strategy of Germany and follows from the *WeGebAu* programme, with the aim to expand access to subsidised training in the context of the digital transformation.

Box 2.2. The German subsidy system to cover training costs in SMEs

The Qualification Opportunities Law came into effect in 2019 and replaces the *WeGebAU Programme*, a successful programme that provided subsidies for training to SMEs and adults with low skills from 2006-19. The Law is part of the new national training strategy of Germany to prepare employees for the digitised world of work, and it aims to improve and widen access to subsidised training to more workers, with particular recognition to the training needs generated by digital transformation.

Under the law, a training activity is eligible for subsidies if it lasts for at least three weeks (or 120 hours) and if workers have at least 3 years of work experience. Training costs are subsidised to varying degrees, depending on size, type of training, worker characteristics, social dialogue and share of employees in need of skill adjustment. The same factors determine if both direct and indirect costs are covered. The training can be administered flexibly, with both part-time and full-time options.

As for direct costs, micro-enterprises (MEs) with less than 10 employees have their training costs fully covered, while large companies with more than 2 500 workers can receive subsidies up to 20% of costs. Similarly, training costs for workers over 45 and people with disabilities in SMEs can be fully covered, as are training costs for low qualified workers who participate in training leading to a qualification. Higher subsidies are also granted when more than 20% of employees in an enterprise require re-training or when the enterprise has a collective agreement in place.

In addition to direct training costs, the subsidy can also cover up to 100% of the wage costs, with coverage rate depending again on firm size, type of training and the workers' qualification levels. In companies with less than 10 employees, reimbursement is set at 75% and can reach 100% if the employee does not possess a vocational qualification. In SMEs (up to 250 employees) reimbursement is set at 50%, but again can increase to 100% if the employee does not have a qualification.

Source: BMAS (2020[17]), *Qualifizierungschancengesetz.*; OECD (2021[18]), *Getting Skills Right: Continuing Education and Training in Germany*, https://dx.doi.org/10.1787/1f552468-en.

In **Denmark**, under the **Arbejdsmarkedsuddannelser (AMU) system** – the Danish system for adult education, costs of training are generally made very low for employers. Companies can benefit from a training subsidy – the Arbejdsgivernes Uddannelsesbidrag (AUB) – to cover wages of staff while in training, in addition to a number of services aimed to support the company throughout the training process, from evaluation of needs to identification of courses and provision of certifications. In addition, employers who want to train their employees benefit from a subsidy for hiring a long-term unemployed as a replacement worker.

According to the Danish **job rotation system**, companies can receive assistance from the PES in identifying replacement workers (unemployed individuals who will take the place of the employees in training) and obtain a hiring subsidy for every hour an employee is on training and an unemployed person works as a substitute. This type of scheme is considered very relevant for SMEs, that are most affected by reduction in the workforce working time in presence of training. In addition, the system both responds to the training needs of companies and supports the reintegration of the unemployed in the labour market. The success of this type of scheme depends on a close collaboration between employers and the PES in order to find the right skill match and on the availability of training for replacement workers where the match is imperfect (OECD, 2020[19]).

Box 2.3. Job Rotation system in Denmark – subsidising replacement workers

Under the Danish system, companies can receive a public subsidy for hiring a long-term unemployed to replace the employee on training, and benefit from public assistance in recruiting such replacement workers. The employment period should last from a minimum of 10 hours to a maximum of 26 weeks, and replacement workers can receive a short training before starting work. Employers receive a hiring subsidy for every hour an employee is on training and an unemployed person is employed as a substitute. The replacement person is selected through the local job centre and receives a wage paid by the employer.

Positive effects are normally registered also for unemployed/replacement workers, who often receive training (a few weeks or longer) in order to fill vacant jobs. The scheme potentially offers a solution to the problem of worker absence for purposes of training, addressing the need to replace the employee, as well as helping the employer meeting the costs of the replacement. The success of this measure, however, is dependent on a close co-operation between a business and the job centre in order to find good skill matches for replacements.

In **Finland**, employers are obliged by law to create training plans for their company. Furthermore, a large supply of training courses is subsidised by public resources. The **Joint Purchase Training system (Yhteishankintakoulutus/ Gemensam anskaffning av utbildning)** is a staff training system, under which training activities are organised by the PES together with individual or groups of employers, who want to retrain existing staff or set-up training programmes for new staff. Employers can receive funding and specific support to find new employees with the right skills or to adapt employees' skills to the company's technological and operational changes.

Box 2.4. The Finnish Joint Purchase Training system

The Joint Purchase Training System is a staff-training programme that supports individual or groups of companies in the delivery of tailored programmes to train newly hired or current employees. Upon the request of the employer, the PES helps the company define its training needs, select the appropriate candidates for training and the right education provider for the delivery of a tailored training, which is also partly funded by the employment services.

Three types of training are subsidised:

- Recruitment Training (RekryKoulutus/ RekryteringsUtbildning) – This type of training is organised with employers who struggle to find employees with the right skills. Employers receive support in developing tailored training, selecting a training provider and recruiting participants for trainings that normally last between 3 and 9 months, with a minimum requirement of 10 days, and should lead to a qualification that allows the individual to perform the required job. The PES co-funds 30% of the costs.
- Tailored Training (TäsmäKoulutus / PrecisionsUtbildning) – This type of training supports employers who want to retrain staff in order to adapt their skills to changing operational or technological landscapes in the company. The minimum duration of the training is of 10 days and the training can take place during a temporary lay-off. This type of training is co-funded by the PES at 50-70% depending on company size. The PES also supports the employers in identifying the employee/s to train and the service provider.

- Change Training (MuutosKoulutus/ OmställningsUtbildning) – This type of training is targeted to workers, more than employers, as it is organised in case of redundancies and supports workers to transition to new jobs, with training that can last between 10 days and two years. Co-funding rate increases to 80% of costs for this type of training.

The Ministry of Economic Affairs and Employment estimates that 3 000 to 4 000 people take part in these types of training every year. According to an evaluation of the programme, this type of support helps employers build a positive learning culture and it is especially relevant for SMEs, which encounter greater challenges in addressing their training and skill needs, even if the minimum duration of 10 days for trainings can constitute a barrier to entry for smaller businesses. Companies were found to be positively affected by the services offered in terms of competence development (OECD, 2020[20]).

The financial incentives above are complemented with measures that build the capacity of companies to identify their training needs and to deliver training. The PES often helps employers define their training needs, select the appropriate candidates for training and find an education provider to deliver the tailored training (OECD, 2019[21]). This type of support also helps employers build a positive learning culture, even if the minimum duration of 10 days for trainings can constitute a barrier to entry for smaller businesses.

Subsidies to human capital cumulation can also be used to respond to sectoral needs, addressing structural changes within the labour market, as well as supporting strategic sectors with strong potential, as it is the case for the digital sector, as shown in the examples below.

MKB!dee is an experimental subsidy scheme launched in the Netherlands and targeting SMEs that encountered difficulties in investing in skills. SMEs that have a good idea to support the development of employees in their company, industry or region can submit an application for a full grant. The scheme has been used to promote projects in technical and ICT sectors, responding to the challenges of digitalisation, climate and green energy transitions, with the aim of strengthening the learning culture in small businesses.

Box 2.5. MKB! Dee – The Netherlands

Started in 2018, MKB! Dee is an experimental subsidy scheme that stimulates SMEs to invest more in training and development. SMEs are asked to propose solutions for barriers encountered when investing in human capital. The full eligible costs of the "solutions" are covered by a grant subsidy.

With MKB! Dee, the Ministry of Economic Affairs and Climate supports entrepreneurs who have a good idea to stimulate the development of employees in their company, industry or region. MKBideenetwerk.nl lists the initiatives and highlights how they give impetus to solutions for skills development. In 2020, 47 ideas were supported. The portal of the initiative also provides an overview of the projects that have received funding and that constitute good examples of different approaches used. In 2019, the scheme was used to promote projects related to technical sectors, energy and climate, and digitalisation. In 2020, funding was aimed at projects that make a contribution to:

- Investments ensuring the availability of personnel in technical and ICT sectors;
- Investments in human capital for digitalisation or for the climate transition; or
- Improvements in the learning culture in small businesses.

The main target group of the programme are SMEs, though industry organisations can also present projects targeting SMEs. If projects are submitted in partnerships, at least 65% of members need to be SMEs.

Source: MKB!DEE (2020[22]), https://mkbideenetwerk.nl/.

2.2. SME vouchers for consulting contracts

Subsidies can be administered through vouchers. Largely used to provide access to training, vouchers can target both employers and employees, and can cover direct and, at times, indirect costs of training.

Employers use vouchers to cover the cost of training for employees. They can purchase vouchers at a discounted price, where the difference between the cost of the service purchased and the SME's disbursement is covered by public funds. Vouchers can be purchased through easy applications, including online, through authorised agencies and intermediaries.

Vouchers are widely used in many European Countries. They have been successfully used as funding schemes for SMEs to invest in digital technologies, innovation and acquisition of high-tech T-shaped skills (European Commission, 2019[23]; European Commission, 2020[24]).[2]

In particular, SME *vouchers for consulting contracts* have been particularly successful in allowing SMEs to innovate by improving their access to high-tech T-shaped skills (see endnote 1). These voucher systems are normally (at least partly) funded by governments, national training funds and/or by enterprises themselves. Consulting companies are usually identified and authorised by the funding agency of the programme, while the system generally includes a government subsidy to be matched by the SME's own resources.

SME vouchers are considered effective as they reach the target group and support the transfer of relevant knowledge to SMEs. The administrative burden for companies is in general low: light procedures are often fully operated online and sometimes dealt with by the consulting companies, thus relieving SMEs from this burden altogether. This type of measure is also considered efficient, with small investments per case and good value for money, and a good level of transferability and scalability. Stakeholders usually report high satisfaction.

Good examples of this type of vouchers are the German 'Go-Inno' and 'Go-Digital' programmes, which are two of several programmes implemented by the German Ministry of Economic Affairs and Energy (BMWi) to support SMEs investing in skills that are relevant for the digital transformation and innovation. Germany has indeed created an SME 4.0 policy strategy, which brings together a large number of policy instruments. Vouchers and subsidies constitute some of the key instruments to fund projects within SMEs.

These programmes are considered successful in developing high-tech skills for SMEs through transfers of technological knowledge and know-how. For the Go-Inno programme, for example, 66% of SMEs stated that only the public funding was the trigger for starting the initiative (European Commission, 2020[24]). Scalability is also considered high, as other companies (both SMEs and consulting organisations) can be easily involved in the voucher scheme.

Transferability is equally considered high: the model offered by the initiatives is highly transferable to different contexts, which is demonstrated by the fact that different national programmes have significant similarities. As a result, the German Go-Digital programme has entered its second phase with more than twice as many expected applicants compared to the first phase (European Commission, 2019[23]).

Overall, this type of measure has a low level of administrative and bureaucratic burden. In addition, funding per case is comparatively small, allowing for the creation of impact already at smaller investments, and for its replication on a large scale with reasonable investments. Furthermore, the fact that SMEs are asked to contribute with own resources (shared funding model) makes the programme more sustainable for public finances. Scaling up best practice funding programmes based on vouchers could therefore respond to the reskilling needs of SMEs.

Box 2.6. Go-Digital and Go-Inno – Vouchers to promote SME Industry 4.0 in Germany

In Germany, innovation and technology funding was consolidated in 2014, and is now managed by the Ministry for Economic Affairs and Energy (BMWi). The policy follows an approached defined as "From idea into the market" to support SMEs, based on four pillars: foundation, competence, pre-competitive research, and market-oriented research and development (R&D). The four pillars are co-ordinated and aim to improve the transfer of technology to SMEs through different programmes. Major and complementary programmes include: Go-Inno, Go-cluster, Mittelstand 4.0-Kompetenzzentren (SME 4.0 Competence Centres), IT-Sicherheit in der Wirtschaft (for IT security), Go-Digital, and the Digital Hub Initiative.

Go-Digital

Among these, the Go-Digital funding programme is a voucher system based on consulting contracts. It supports SMEs and craft businesses that want to optimise their business processes with the help of digital solutions. SMEs are supported by consulting firms, which provide the individual company with professional advice and support in implementing innovative measures, setting up or improving on modern technological systems. The programme covers three modules: 'digitised business processes', 'digital market development' and 'IT security', granting SMEs tailored advice that responds to their specific needs on these three topics. It targets German-based SMEs that have fewer than 100 employees and a turnover (of the previous year) under EUR 20 million.

The consulting companies are pre-authorised by the BMWi, following an application that can be filled out electronically and digitally signed. In order to be authorised the consulting companies need to be a legally independent, prove economic stability for the past three years, guarantee competition-neutral advice, give proof of technical expertise, provide references to small business advisory clients, co-operate with universities and research institutions and fulfil the quality standards set by the programme. EuroNorm GmbH, a service company that works as management agency for the programme, then reviews the application. The decision normally takes force after 4 weeks from approval, when the company is included in the list of pre-approved consultancies that SMEs can contact. Consultancies have also the option to address SMEs directly.

The request for funding is preceded by a meeting between company and consultants, which is followed by the conclusion of a consulting contract that specifies the services to be carried out, for which prescribed contract templates are provided. The consulting company proceeds then to initiate the process, taking on all formalities linked to the projects – from the application for funding, which is made online, to the proof of use. This allows for easy access to funding for SMEs and relief of administrative burden. The application must be accompanied by a description of the project, which includes its economic effects. The consulting company assumes overall responsibility of the project and has a number of obligations, such as to review the eligibility of the SME and to document the provision of the services and use of funding, whose proof of use must be submitted within 4 weeks from the project's completion.

The costs are subsidised at 50%. The maximum duration of each funding grant is 30 days over a period of six months, with a maximum coverage of EUR 16 500 per project and a maximum daily consultant rate of EUR 1 100. Eligible funding varies depending on number and type of services chosen. The beneficiary company has the contractual obligation to pay its own share and to allow success controls by the BMWi. It also confirms the provided services on the proof of use and evaluates the quality of the advice.

The programme has an overall budget for the initiative of EUR 10 million per year. It is considered attractive for SMEs and being an online programme with low level of bureaucracy and application effort.

It is complementary to the work of Mittelstand 4.0 Competence Centres that give general advice to SMEs.

The website of the WBMi beyond including detailed information and guidance on the programme, also include practical examples of how the programme has benefited SMEs and craft businesses. Importantly, the programme has been used to respond to the needs of companies in terms of work adaptation, because of the COVID-19 pandemic. Companies can now receive financial support if they create home office jobs at short notice. The Go-Digital programme has been expanded and tested to cover these needs through a 4th module for setting up home workspaces, covering individual advice and the implementation of these solutions, such as setting of software and configuration of hardware.

Go-Inno

Similarly to Go-Digital, the Go-Inno programme is a voucher-system, tailored this time to innovation and marketing. Small companies often lack the knowledge of the latest methods and instruments to manage product innovations or technical process innovations internally. The Go-Inno programme aims to increase the innovative strength and competitiveness of the companies, with qualified external advice that helps in the preparation and implementation of ideas related to innovation.

As for the Go-Digital programme, the delivery of funding is mediated by consulting companies, which give tailored advice to SMEs. The BMWi authorises consulting companies through a management agency (the German Aerospace Centre), which reviews applications on the basis of a number of requirements: the consulting firms has at least three consultants with a broad spectrum of innovation and technological skills; they offer a non-competitive, branch and technology-open advice on innovation projects, as shown by references; they have expertise to offer comprehensive innovation advice, beyond engineering and scientific qualifications; they have experience in co-operating with universities and research institutions; have knowledge of federal and state funding for technology and innovation and are able to inform the beneficiary companies about public funding; they satisfy quality standards of the programme. The consulting companies must also have good knowledge of the target group. Authorisation only takes place after two projects have been carried out successfully, while until then the company is only provisionally authorised. Companies that do not generate a project in 12 months need to reapply for authorisation. The selection procedure used for consulting companies has proved effective, with a very high rate of satisfaction among SMEs on the work of consulting companies.

The programme funds services related to (i) potential analysis, an examination of the company profile with regard to innovation project, marketability, capacity requirements and financing plan, or (ii) implementation and/or project management of the concept. It targets SMEs located in Germany with less than 100 employees and an annual turnover of less than EUR 20 million. Funding is generally provided without thematic restriction to specific technologies, products, branches or sectors of economy, though agriculture and fisheries are not eligible under this scheme. Subsidies are at 50%, with a maximum daily consultant rate of EUR 1 100. The maximum length/cost of the project depends on the service to be offered: 10 working days for potential analysis (max EUR 5 500); 25 days for realisation of the concept (max EUR 13 750); 15 days for the management of the project (max EUR 8 250).

The consulting company checks the SME's eligibility for funding and relieves it from all formalities. The SME is contractually obliged to take part in the project actively, make its financial contribution and confirming the consultancy's work is in line with what agreed. The SME also assesses the quality of the work provided.

2.3. Tax incentives

Tax incentives have been equally used to support investment in training and hiring of new talent. Tax incentives include: tax allowances, which are deducted from gross income to arrive at taxable income; tax exemptions, in which income is exempted from the taxable base; tax credits, where sums are detected from the taxes due; and tax deferrals, which are the postponement of tax payment (OECD, 2017[3]).

Overall, tax measures have the advantage that they build on institutional arrangements that already exist; hence, they come at relatively low cost for employers and policy makers (OECD, 2017[3]). Tax incentives can be used to target training, give leeway to employers to decide who and how to train, and are appreciated by employers for their low administrative burden (Cedefop, 2009[25]). However, tax incentives generally require high incentives, and generate high deadweight losses, as they can be used to finance investments that would have been performed by the firm even in absence of public support (Stone, 2010[16]).

Moreover, tax credits are usually available to all companies, short of constituting a form of state aid as regulated by national and international competition law. As such, they do not favour disadvantaged groups or small companies in particular (Cedefop, 2009[25]). SMEs can benefit of higher rates or deductions, with differential rates based on firm size or conditional on having previously invested in training already. Extending the list of expenses covered by the incentive, and in particular including the salary of workers in training, would also benefit SMEs disproportionately, and so do simplified funding application procedures. Even so, careful design is needed for these types of incentives to act as a stimulus for SMEs, balancing deadweight expenditure and administrative costs. However, closer targeting rapidly increases the administrative burden on public authorities. For these reasons, tax incentives should be considered mainly a supplementary measure for SMEs, which needs to be accompanied by other instruments to achieve good outcomes.

2.4. Payback clauses

One of the core risks of investing in training is poaching, i.e. that the employee leaves the company shortly after the termination of training. This risk can be higher for small businesses, in light of their higher overall cost of training on average (Cedefop, 2012[26]).

Payback clauses are a means of overcoming this risk and thus indirectly promoting training investment. When a payback clause applies, an employee who has undergone training and terminates an employment relationship within a set contractual retention period, has to refund (part of the) training costs to the employer. The clause and the regulations constituting its legal foundations dictate which costs need to be covered in case of reimbursement, the progressive reduction of the reimbursement as time passes, and the applicable contractual retention period.

The conditions of the clauses can be regulated at the national level by law, in collective agreements between social partners, or at the company level, in individual contracts of employment or in training agreements. Overall, payback clauses exist in most European countries with a variety of modalities (Cedefop, 2012[26]). Regulations in collective agreements at sectoral level or in companies seem however a more suitable approach, allowing the rules on payback clauses to adapt better to sector/branch or the company and employee training needs. Unlike national regulations, they can target the needs of a particular sector and be more specific with regard to the costs to be covered, the progressive reduction of the reimbursement and the retention period.

Importantly, these clauses can make both parties aware of their responsibility to provide and participate in training, and they can motivate employers to increase investment in employee training while reducing the risk linked to it. At the same time, the clause needs to be specific on the type of training and coverage to avoid excessive restrictions on employee's mobility. As the content of training needs to be described in the contract between worker and firm, payback clauses are more adequate for training programs with clearly specified content and/or yielding a certification that guarantees the quality of the training provided. A second limitation of these measures is the credibility of the worker's promise to pay: a cash-constrained worker is not able to reimburse the firm's cost of training upon leaving. This limitation is usually overcome by requiring the poaching firm to step in and provide the amount due. Lastly, attention should be given to the ability of enforcing the clause at the judiciary level: excessive enforcement costs (e.g. lengthy trials) are likely to reduce the uptake by SMEs in particular.

The system in the **Netherlands** can be considered an inspiring example and a suitable model. In the country, regulations define conditions in collective agreements at sectoral and company levels. Most of Dutch agreements with provisions on vocational training include also payback clauses that respond to the needs of the branch or company. Payback clauses that are triggered if the employee does not complete the training can provide workers with an incentive to complete the course, as is the case in most agreements in the country.

2.5. Recognising the costs of informal training

SMEs are generally found to prefer informal learning (learning by doing, learning from peers and supervisors while performing one's job) to formal training, as the former is typically less costly (Cedefop, 2015[27]). This form of training, however, is not normally covered by subsidies or financial incentives. Recognising the cost linked to informal learning actions in addition to formal and non- formal training costs can therefore be an interesting approach to incentivise investment in skills by SMEs (Stone, 2010[16]).

The **AFEST – Action de formation en situation de travail (Learning at the workplace)** was developed in France to provide some level of formalisation and structure to on-the-job informal training, allowing firms and workers to access certain financial incentives that are normally reserved for organised forms of training. The measure targets SMEs and micro companies and covers costs linked to informal learning actions in addition to formal and non- formal training costs. By doing so, the initiative includes informal on-the-job training under the training funded by the levy system in place in France, extending the scope of coverage and ultimately facilitating access to funding to firms that would be otherwise left out (European Commission, 2020[24]).

Box 2.7. AFEST – Action de formation en situation de travail – France

The launch of the experimentation of the AFEST was decided in 2014 by the General Delegation for employment and vocational training (DGEFP, Délégation Générale à l'emploi et à la formation professionnelle) of the Ministry of Labour. The AFEST targets medium, small and micro companies, as well as low-qualified people who are frequently excluded from formal training.

Before starting the training spell on the job, the employee and the employer are asked to determine its objectives and the skills they would like to develop. They need to prove that the training in practice would have a positive impact on skills acquisition.

An official from an OPCO can be involved at this stage to help the employee and the employer determine the objectives and the skills to acquire. OPCO are French competence operators that accompany SMEs in the definition of their training needs. They operate since 2019, when they replaced the OPCAs (Organismes Paritaires Collecteurs Agréées) in this function. As OPCAs, they are bodies governed jointly by employers and employees, but do not have the function of training funds as OPCAs did. Today there are in France 11 OPCOs, which include about 330 professional branches and they aim at: financing apprenticeship, helping branches to build professional certifications; provide technical support to professional branches for SAA exercises (so called gestion prévisionnelle de l'emploi et des competences GPEC). In addition, they work to provide a service to very small, small and medium-sized enterprises, allowing for improvements in the information and access of these companies to vocational training; and to support these companies in the analysis and definition of their professional training needs, particularly with regard to economic and technical changes in their sector of activity.

The impact of the AFEST on decreasing barriers to training provision in small and micro companies is substantial, especially since it addresses challenges such as lack of time, financial cost and inadequacy of training. AFEST also has a positive impact on low-qualified employees by providing tailored training. These beneficial effects led policy makers to scale up the measure, which was ratified by law in 2018.

Source: Anact-Aract (2018[28]), *Expérimentation Afest – Action de Formation En Situation de Travail: Rapport Final ;* Sgarzi, (2019[29]), *Upskilling pathways in France*, CEREQ.

3 Building SMEs' capacity and learning culture

SMEs face challenges to training and hiring new talent that go beyond the costs of such activities and are rather linked to the firms' capacity to invest in the acquisition and effective use of relevant skills.

Indeed, relative to large firms, SMEs have less information on the existing opportunities for training and for support to training available to them; in other cases, they are not aware that training is needed, as they lack the capacity to assess their skill needs; and in other cases still, they enjoy lower levels of trust or awareness about the benefits of training, or simply the long-term business perspective which is needed to invest in human capital and innovation (OECD, 2019[21]).

These relative deficiencies often stem from the firm's lack of a professional human resource department or of specialised staff, which are dedicated to organise and co-ordinate training, assess personnel's needs, navigate the landscape of available funding and trainings, or more broadly develop tools to attract new talent or upskill the current workforce (OECD, 2020[19]).

In other cases, SMEs' ability to invest in human capital crucially relies on the skills and vision of the company's management. Measures that promote innovative management practices and workplace innovation, build management and leadership skills, and promote a culture of learning are instrumental to enhance investment in and the effective utilisation of skills within SMEs.

For these reasons, effective policies combine both financial support and measures aimed to enhance SMEs' access to these functions as provided by external providers, or their capacity to develop them within the company itself.

3.1. Skill assessment and anticipation capacity

The effective use of skills in a firm requires that skill needs are regularly assessed and anticipated. Building the capacity to do so remains one of the main challenges they face when it comes to investment in human capital. While approximately 68% of firms in the EU27 report having performed a diagnosis of skill needs in 2015 (CVTS), a large proportion of them only do so irregularly, and do not align training activities with the resulting skill priorities (OECD, 2019[2]). Managers struggle to identify the skill needs of the firm, especially beyond the short-term, and the training programmes that may address them (OECD, 2017[3]).

Skill assessment and anticipation (SAA) exercises are tools to generate information about the current and future skills needs of the firm (or more generally of labour market), and the available supply. These exercises can be found in all OECD countries, at the national, regional or sectoral level, and are carried out mostly by public bodies or within tripartite networks. The main aim of these exercises is to inform relevant stakeholders about how to align demand and supply of skills within the changing labour market, and help them plan for the future (OECD, 2016[30]).

Generally, the PES in each country is an important actor in enabling skill assessment and anticipation, facilitating the matching of skill supply and demand through dissemination of information and active support services to companies and job seekers (OECD, 2016[30]).

At the regional and sectoral level, **participatory approaches that involve social partners** can have a positive effect on employer awareness with regard to skill needs and trends, as well as on and training supply. This is the case of *Skill Councils or Fora*, where stakeholders discuss skill-related issues and provide recommendations on relevant policies, including on the monitoring and forecasting of competence needs in their sector or region (OECD, 2016[30]). The Irish Network of Regional Skills Fora, for example, help regional public partners and businesses identify skill needs, and the education and training system shape adequate responses.

Box 3.1. SAA and support to employers in Ireland

Skills councils are employer-led or tri-partite organisations involving representatives from employers, workers and government or educational institutions. They are usually independent organisations that provide a platform for the discussion of skills-related challenges of specific sectors or regional areas, as well as the development of joint policy responses. One of their tasks is to monitor the labour market in the relevant sector and forecast which skills will be needed.

In Ireland, for example, Regional Skills Fora help regional public partners and businesses identify skill needs, and the education and training system shape adequate responses, in nine regions. More specifically they provide:

- A contact point in each region to help employers connect with services and supports available across the education and training system;
- Robust labour market information and analysis of employer needs;
- Greater collaboration and utilisation of resources across the education and training system;
- A structure for employers to become more involved in promoting employment and opportunities for career progression in their sectors.

A Regional Skills Website was launched in May 2016 as a communication tool for employers and education and training providers. The website provides access to a detailed profile for each of the nine Regions drawn from all relevant skills research and datasets to provide the basis for informed dialogue on skills needs.

The work plan of RSF within each region is driven by key stakeholders including employers, enterprises and education and training providers. The RSF engage with all sectors and size of businesses, but have a particular focus on SMEs, with 55% of all activity focusing on small businesses in 2019.

Within this context, in 2018 the 'Skills for Growth' project was launched, providing a service for employers to help them identify their skill needs and receive guidance on education and training providers best suited for them. Each employer in the programme had access to a skills audit tool to capture data on the skill needs of their business; as well as, one to one assistance from a RFS Manager to use this tool and plan for the future. Once skill needs are identified, Regional Skills Fora link companies with education and training providers.

Enterprise Ireland – A government agency in Ireland responsible for supporting Irish businesses – is also involved in the programme and runs a series of 'Spotlight on Skills' tailored workshops for companies. In those workshops, the companies gain knowledge on human resources and skills management.

This is an collaborative project led by the Department of Education and Skills and Enterprise Ireland, working in partnership with Regional Skills Fora Managers as well as SOLAS – the national agency responsible for further education and training, under the Department of Education and Skills, in addition to other stakeholders, such as the Higher Education Institutions that are part of the Mid-East North Dublin (MEND) cluster, the All Ireland Research Observatory (AIRO).

Source: OECD (2016[30]), *Getting Skills Right: Assessing and Anticipating Skill Needs*, OECD Publishing, https://doi.org/10.1787/9789264252073-en; Irish Department of Education and Skills, (2020[31]), *Regional Skills Fora – Annual Report 2019*; Regional Skills Forum, (2020[32]), *Skills for Growth*.

While these exercises are instrumental to influence policies and to inform workers about the skills in highest demand on the market, **SAAs at the company level** remains rare, especially for SMEs (OECD, 2016[30]). At the company level, different approaches can be used to help SMEs improve their skill assessment and anticipation capacity. Often programmes that promote subsidised training, such as the ones presented in Chapter 2, also provide SMEs with support in the identification of their training needs, of the right candidates for training and of the most relevant training options. Similarly, in the context of the digital transformation, programmes that help SMEs build their digitalisation strategies can also offer support in the identification of skill needs.

SMEs can access SAA services as performed by an external party, or develop their own internal capacity to perform such an assessment. Public support measures can target either form. This section is mainly concerned with the internal development of SMEs' capacity: programmes that help SMEs develop HR structures and competences, as well as programmes that build the capacity of managers to assess the needs of their company, and programmes that promote workplace innovation and improved management practices.

Box 3.2. The Forecast management agreement for jobs and skills (GPEC) – France

Advance management for jobs and skills (*Gestion prévisionnelle des emplois et des compétences* – GPEC) is an instrument for strategic workforce planning embedded in French labour law. It brings together aspects of skills analysis and skills planning at the aggregate level with processes of human resources management at the company level.

The purpose of the GPEC is to anticipate, in the short and medium term, human resources needs in companies and to feed them into the collective bargaining process. For the company, it translates into the obligation to perform a global diagnosis of its employees' skills and abilities, based on individual reviews and reviews of skills and professional experiences.

However, the GPEC goes beyond the collection of information and aims to prepare employees for these changes. Several tools can be used at the employee level: individual performance review, validation of professional experience acquired on the job (VAE) but also training. GPEC medium-term objective is to adapt jobs, staffing levels and skills to the requirements of corporate strategy and changes in its economic, social and legal environment. It is a prospective human resources management tool that is expected to support change(s) within a company.

In France GPEC is now mandatory for companies with more than 300 employees. For SMEs, state aid is available and companies with small HR departments can work with consultancies specialised on implementing GPEC.

Assistance can be provided by DIRECCTE, the French regional directorates for companies, competition, consumption, labour and employment under the Ministry of Labour, which are unique interlocutors at the regional level for businesses and socio-economic actors and bring together administrative services from various backgrounds. Through DIRECCTE, SMEs can access assistance for human resources consultancy services can be applied to an individual company or a group of companies in the same branch, sector and territory, and subject to the same HR issues. Support can be provided for a maximum of 20 consulting days on themes related to the integration of HR into the company or the professionalisation of the HR function for both leaders and management. The maximum amount of the subsidy for each company is of EUR 15 000 excluding tax, with the remaining 50% of the cost borne by the company, in case of individual support. Support to groups of companies is limited to EUR12 500 with a maximum coverage of 90% of costs. The cost of using software for SAA from private providers can also be financed within the framework of aid to companies.

Source: Ministère du Travail, de l'Emploi et de l'Insertion (2014[33]), *Gestion prévisionnelle de l'emploi et des compétences (GPEC)*; European Commission (2018[34]), *Skills audits: tools to identify talent*.

Dissemination of SAA results carried out at national regional and sectoral level is also important. In most countries, results from SAA exercises are shared and disseminated through the publication of reports and the development of websites. Public media (TV, radio, newspapers or magazines) and in more rare cases (e.g. in the Netherlands), social media are also used to disseminate the results (OECD, 2016[30]). Effective web dissemination usually centralises all the information on one platform. Web platforms are particularly successful when they have more than one interface depending on the targeted audience or when they allow for an interactive experience. This is the case, for example, in Austria, with the "Qualification Barometer" web platform (OECD, 2018[35]).

3.2. Promoting innovative and modern workplace practices

Work organisation, job design and management practices are important factors in influencing skills use. Modern human resource management, High-Performance Working Practices (HPWP) and workplace innovation therefore play an important role in ensuring effective skill utilisation within companies, with clear effects on performance and competiveness, as well as quality of life and work experience for employees.[3]

The promotion of HPWP however is not solely motivated by skills utilisation. Several countries have undertaken initiatives to promote changes within these areas, with policy efforts motivated by a variety of objectives, including innovation, productivity and job quality (OECD, 2020[15]).

The German Federal Government, for instance, is taking various approaches to build the capacity of SMEs to develop HR and personnel policies that can make SMEs attractive and innovative employers in light of current economic and labour market trends. In particular, the 2014-20 European Social Fund (ESF) programming has been largely leveraged at federal level to build the capacity of SMEs in this respect.

KOFA is the German **Competence Centre on Securing Skilled Labour** that assists SMEs in their efforts to become and remain attractive employers and stay competitive on the labour market. The Centre is funded by the BMWi and ESF and operates as an online platform that supports SMEs in their HR work, targeting mainly directors and HR managers in SMEs, and providing instruments for innovative and modern human resources.

The measure facilitates knowledge sharing and dissemination and provides recommendations and best practice examples, but also workshops and trainings, and online tools to assess the company situation and HR functions. It supports SMEs HR capacity and makes information easy to access and understand, with very operational approaches and examples, which are key for supporting SMEs understanding and integrating new solutions (OECD, 2020[19]).

Box 3.3. Competence Centre on securing skilled labour (KOFA) – Germany

The "Competence Centre on securing skilled labour" (KOFA) operates an online platform to support small and medium-sized companies in their HR work. Its aim is to assist SMEs in their efforts to become attractive as employers and remain competitive by recruiting, training and retaining staff. KOFA is a project of the Cologne Institute for Economic Research and is funded by the Federal Ministry for Economic Affairs and Energy. It aims to attract SMEs, and motivate them to implement modern and skill-enhancing HR practices.

More specifically, KOFA offers the following: studies (analyses of the skilled worker situation in Germany), recommendations for action and checklists on HR work, practical and best practice examples, information and guidance on future trends, such as digital education and leadership 4.0, lectures and networks, with exchange with experts, and webinars for remote training and exchange. The website contains welcome guides, step-by-step guides, with checklists and recommendations for actions, that guide SMEs through analysis of company needs and current situation, strategic HR work, in addition to dossiers on topics such as digitalisation in SMEs, digital education and training, training 4.0, digital teachings and learning methods, and inclusion in SMEs of migrant/refugee workers.

KOFA's offer is primarily aimed at managing directors and HR managers in SMEs. For companies, KOFA provides instruments for innovative and modern human resources along the entire production chain, from situation and company analysis to positioning as an employer to finding, retaining and qualifying specialised workers.

With reference to the latter, the Centre supports the initiative "Custom-made appointments" (*Passgenaue Besetzung*) of the Federal Ministry for Economic Affairs and Energy. The project helps SMEs find suitable trainees and specialists, by filling vacant positions and training, including through foreign skilled workers and migrants already living in Germany. The project makes use of a network of about 160 consultants that work with the companies throughout the process of recruitment. It is funded by the BMWI and the ESF, with companies contributing 30% of the costs. The project is running since 2007, with around 100 000 training positions and more than 10 000 positions for entry-level qualification successfully filled. The initiative will be extended by a further three years until the end of 2023.

In addition, the KOFA benchmark tool *Spiegel der Personalpolitik* offers companies an interactive comparison of their own HR work with other companies. With a quick check, companies can analyse the situation of their company in a few minutes and find out whether there is a need for action.

The design of personnel policies that can help SMEs respond to current mega-trends in the labour market such as digitalisation and globalisation is further supported by the German Government and the European Social Fund through two programmes: the **UnternehmensWert: Mensch (uMV)** programme, that aims to support SMEs and their employees in designing employee-oriented and future-oriented personnel policies, and the **Fachkräfte sichern** programme, which aims to support the establishment of staff development and training structures within small companies.

In particular, the uMV programme focuses on promoting the development of personnel policies within SMEs through a tripartite approach and along four main areas of HR policy that are considered strategic for the future of companies: personnel management, equal opportunities and diversity, health, knowledge and competences. The programme supports the initiation of change processes related to organisational development through a three-stage, participation-oriented advisory process, which is geared to the needs of companies and works through counselling centres and process consulting vouchers. The 102 contact points, or counselling centres *(EBS),* carry out an initial consultation with the company, with the aim to check eligibility and needs. Based on this consultation, the EBS can emit a voucher that allows SMEs to access further consulting services for a maximum of 10 days (BMAS, 2020[36]).

To date, the programme has served about 5 000 companies, scaling up after a successful pilot scheme, that showed high levels of company satisfaction and overall high participation of employees and a high share of companies undertaking follow-up measures at their own expenses in order to continue the processes initiated (BMAS, 2020[36]). Since 2017, the programme (called *uMV Plus*) has also been used to support SMEs developing **learning and experimenting rooms,** projects in which new approaches to solving the challenges of the future of work are tested in operational practice, with a strong focus on digital change, smart transformation and, since 2019, Artificial Intelligence. The uMV programme seems scalable and transferrable to other contexts, with low levels of administrative burden for SMEs, which are supported by counselling centres, as was the case for voucher systems leveraging on consulting companies and aiming at building digitalisation capacity.

Box 3.4. Ensuring skilled labour in SMEs through the ESF – Germany

The initiative "Securing the skilled labour base: vocational training and education (CVET) and gender equality" (Fachkräfte sichern: weiterbilden und Gleichstellung fördern) supports social partners and companies' management in securing the supply of skilled labour. It does so by establishing sustainable training structures and personnel development strategies, increasing participation in adult training in SMEs, strengthening the learning culture in the company, and improving career advancement and opportunities for women and generally gender equality at work. For this purpose, actions fundable under the programme include:

- Creation of staff development structures: concepts for personnel development (e.g. development of qualification plans, introduction of diversity management); upgrading the skills of key individuals in companies (e.g. specialists and managers, personnel managers, members of company interest groups) to become training multipliers, and implementing concepts for adapting qualification to increasing and changing requirements of technological innovation, especially in the area of the green economy; implementation of concepts to promote learning in work processes;
- Development of training advisory structures for SMEs and creation/implementation of in-company and inter-company training measures for SMEs;
- Initiation of social dialogue: workshops of social partners to initiate and conclude agreements on qualification and equal opportunities in the sector; analysis of sectoral needs for training and gender equality polices; determination of needs for future competence profiles; strategies, concepts and projects for developing industry standards with regard to further training and equality;
- Strengthening the competences of operational actors with regard to equal opportunities: advice and qualification for company interest groups; sensitisation and coaching of executives and HR managers; development and implementation of guidelines or company agreements for the improvement of the employment situation of women; promotion of equal participation of women and men in working life;
- Development of work time models and career pathway plans geared towards specific phases in a worker's life: development and implementation of innovative approaches to the organisation of working hours to improve the workforce participation of women, taking into account business needs and work-life balance; approaches to reduce loss of qualifications of employees when on parental leave and support to quick career re-entry.

The programme is a joint initiative of the Federal Ministry of Labour and Social Affairs (BMAS), the Confederation of German Employers' Associations and the Confederation of German Trade Unions, with around EUR 130 million in funds from the BMAS, the European Social Fund and contributions from companies and social partners. It is the follow-up programme to the "Further Education" (*Weiter bilden*) and "Equal opportunities" (*Gleichstellen*) programmes, that were implemented in 2007-13 ESF programming period.

Under these initiatives, more than 93 projects were successfully funded, including projects aiming at developing structures and skills linked to smart transformation, digitalisation and entrepreneurship. Guidelines are developed and implemented in close collaboration with the partners, with collective agreements on training or agreements with social partners on skills development and equal opportunities being a prerequisite for project funding.

The **"UnternehmensWert: Mensch**" (**uMV**) programme aims to support SMEs and their employees in designing an employee-oriented and future-oriented personnel policy, on the basis of a holistic and tripartite approach developed within the framework of the New Quality of Work initiative launched by the German Government. The programme is aimed at supporting the development of human resource policies that are in line with current mega-trends. In particular it focuses on four areas which are considered strategic for HR policy and the future of companies:

- Personnel management: modern personnel management which takes into consideration the individual needs of employees, with a participatory approach to decisions;
- Equal opportunities and diversity: creating policies that consider the specifics of the company own workforce and offer all employees development opportunities, regardless of age, gender, family or cultural background;
- Health: creating offers suitable to promote physical and mental health and increasing awareness of employees;
- Knowledge and competence: developing ways to incentivise knowledge sharing and learning within the company, in addition to providing specific training to respond to digital transformation and measures to promote employee motivation to learn.

The federal programme supports the initiation of change processes related to organisational development, supplementing programmes at the State (regional) level.

The programme was launched after the implementation of a successful pilot programme and provides for a three-stage, participation-oriented advisory process that is specifically geared to the needs of the companies. There are 102 main contact points for the programme – so-called *counselling centres* (EBS) – that carry out the initial consultation, accompany SMEs with red tape, carry out public relations, and provide guidance for other regional support instruments for SMEs.

As part of the initial consultation, the counselling centres verify eligibility and, together with the companies, identify the specific operational changes required needs along the four areas of human resource policy of the programme (personnel management, equal opportunities and diversity, health, knowledge and skills). Depending on the results of this consulting phase, companies and their employees can have access to further advice to the extent of a maximum of ten consultation days. This second consultation focuses on production processes, takes place directly on site, and is performed by consultants specialised in operation management. It includes the analysis of the company's strengths and weaknesses, as well as the development of action goals and measures, which are then recorded in a binding operational action plan. The suggested change in processes is then initiated and accompanied. Six months after the second consulting, the initial counselling centre with the participation of the social partners at company level or individual employees assesses the implemented measures. In this occasion, the EBS checks whether there is a need for further advice and whether the company can request access to other State-wide support measures.

By 2019 around 4 900 small companies had taken advantage of these consulting services.

In addition to the above, since 2017, the ESF programme can be used to fund the creation and set up of learning and experimenting rooms (*Lern- und Experimentierräume*). In line with the White Paper on Work 4.0 and the initiative "Sustainable Companies and Administrations in Digital Change" (*Zukunftsfähige Unternehmen und Verwaltungen im digitalen Wandel*), companies and administrations can set up and apply for funding to create learning and experimentation rooms. These test new approaches to solving the challenges of the future of work in operational practice, with a strong focus on digital change, smart transformation and Artificial intelligence. In particular through the uMV Plus programme, SMEs that have been on the market for at least two years can receive support in the development of experimentation rooms from trained process consultants, with the aim to support them in the adoption of digital technologies. The funding covers 80% of 12 consultation days.

The initiative is linked to an online platform for practice and transfer www.experimentierraeume.de, which provides companies and administrations with an online space to present their learning and exchange ideas with other companies. Experts from science, business and trade unions also comment on various aspects of digitalisation.

Source: BMAS (2020[37]), *Initiative Fachkräfte sichern.*

When considering workplace innovation and innovative personnel policies, Nordic countries have a long tradition of workplace development programmes. While these programmes can respond to a variety of policy priorities (e.g. innovation, growth, quality of life) they generally encourage training and learning, as well as an effective use of skills within the company. Many of these programmes, however, depend on the national and regional context to be effective. **InnovaSouth** is a project that aims to support workplace innovation in SMEs in the South of Europe, wanting to improve the entrepreneurial culture of small companies in the region and move beyond the challenges specific to them.

The project, which has been funded through Horizon 2020, provides services and financial support for innovative workplace solutions, including a *manual of good practices*, which can be used by SMEs to understand and put in practice easy solutions that promote employee's motivation and productivity, as well as an online questionnaire to assess how innovative workplace are.

Box 3.5. InnovaSouth

InnovaSouth is a project funded by Horizon 2020, which aims to improve Southern European SMEs' entrepreneurial culture, while increasing their resilience and competitiveness, through the provision of services and financial support for innovative workplace solutions. The project is based on a matrix of best practices related to four fundamental drivers of innovation: jobs and teams; organisational structures, management and procedures; employee driven improvement and innovation; co-created leadership and horizontal structure.

For each of these categories, workplace innovation practices are identified, distinguishing between practices that can be carried out for free and those that involve spending of resources.

One of the tools of the project is an **online manual of good practices** for workplace innovation, available in various languages. It aims to inspire entrepreneurs to find simple and innovative solutions to increase employee's motivation and productivity. The Online Manual is aimed at SMEs that need practical advice on possible innovation actions to implement within their companies. It includes monetary and non-monetary solutions to promote workplace innovation, including for example practices on how to promote transversal skills among employees, with description of exercises that can be carried out in the workplace and practical examples implemented in other companies.

In addition, an online questionnaire is also available for companies to assess their level of workplace innovation. The questionnaire is available in different languages (Italian, Greek, English) and includes 20 questions.

InnovaSouth also provides SMEs with a EUR 8 000 voucher to be spent on workplace innovation services.

Source: InnovaSouth (2020[38]), https://www.innovasouthproject.eu/methodology/.

3.2.1. Workforce innovation diagnostic tools

Diagnostic tools and self-assessment surveys provide an affordable way for companies to assess their current work organisation and needs. These tools can be built with different objectives, helping companies and employers to assess their needs with regard to skills and professional development specifically, or within the broader context of workplace innovation or even digital maturity. The practices below provide good examples of instruments that respond to these different objectives. They include tools that can be administered online or in person to companies, mostly thanks to surveys and in-person interviews.

The **Workplace Innovation Tool** in **Ireland** is an online questionnaire that facilitates a business in self-evaluation of its capacity to become a more innovative workplace. The service is designed to enable single individuals within an organisation to participate; each asks a number of questions about the organisation, with regard to employee engagement, innovation, productivity and training approaches. The tool produces an individual report and a company report, that can provide the basis for an assessment of the strengths and weaknesses of the business, and a starting point as how to best enhance the business's capability to prepare, adapt and respond to change.

Box 3.6. The Workplace Innovation Tool – Ireland

The Workplace Innovation Tool focuses on employee engagement, innovation, productivity and training. The toolkit encourages businesses to be proactive in transforming their work practices by quickly identifying areas for improvement. It then guides users to relevant supports.

It is composed of an online questionnaire of 25 questions designed around four pillars: employee engagement, innovation, productivity and training. An unlimited number of employees in an organisation can participate. Each is asked a number of questions about his/her organisation's approaches to Employee Engagement, Innovation, Productivity and Training. The whole process takes only a matter of minutes and everyone receives a personalised report with signposting to relevant, high quality events and resources to help drive change. The report suggests opportunities for job rotation, training, or mentorship within the firm based on the employee's inputted skills, interests and experience.

The toolkit produces two reports: a personalised report for each individual respondent, and a company report (generated only if there are two or more respondents). The company report shows the average result for the company's individual respondents. It provides the basis to assess the strengths and weaknesses of the business and can be used to start the conversation on how best to enhance the business's capability to prepare, adapt and respond to change. The personal report enables individual respondents to assess their strengths and weaknesses under the four aforementioned pillars.

The Workplace Innovation Toolkit is a 2018 governmental initiative involving: National Government, Department of Business, Enterprise and Innovation, Regional/local government Local Enterprise Offices, Employer or employee organisations, the foreign investment promotion agency (IDA Ireland), the investment and export promotion agency (Enterprise Ireland), Skillnet Ireland, a union-based research institute on workplace innovation (Ideas Institute), the quasi-governmental commission for employment relations (Workplace Relations Commission) and the National Standards Authority of Ireland, which decides on certifications including on management practices.

This instrument has been developed and is supported by the social partners (government, trade unions and employer organisations, and other state bodies such as the Workplace Relations Commission), which fosters the buy-in from its constituents.

Source: https://witool.dbei.gov.ie.

Similarly, **Workplace Innovation Europe**, a non-profit organisation focusing on workplace innovation in Europe, offers a pay-for diagnostic tool in the form of an employee survey, designed to employers an in-depth understanding of where change is needed and how to deliver it. The tool focuses on evidence-based workplace practices associated with high performance, engagement and workforce health, and the reporting indicates specific actions at team, department, site and organisational levels. (Workplace Innovation Europe, 2020[39]) The organisation offers different pricing and services for micro-, small and medium-sized organisations, as well as a free version of the toolkit.

Other diagnostic tools have been developed to support SMEs in assessing their level of maturity with regard to specific aspects such as the digital transformation. These tools are often provided by private sector or by research organisations. In France, The "Smart Diag' tool", for example, is a 5-minute survey that aims to help SMEs identify their level of digital maturity, including areas of strength and weakness, pointing out areas where further progress can be made and identifying potential follow-up services. The tool was launched in 2018, as part of a larger initiative, the Smart SME Initiative, which also offers support services to SMEs, including training for digital upgrading and development of training plans for employees (OECD, 2020[40]). The **European Digital SME Alliance** maintains a repertory of tools available to SMEs for self-assessment (European Digital SME Alliance, 2020[41]).

3.2.2. Remote work

The COVID-19 crisis promoted the use of remote-work technologies in a large number of firms across OECD countries. In many instances, remote work was the only feasible way for the firm to keep on producing while respecting social distancing and stay-at-home mandates. Even beyond the pandemic emergency, some of the investments companies made in upgrading their digital tools and organisational structure are likely to remain relevant and affect firms' skills requirements and reskilling practices (OECD, 2021[8]).

SMEs were especially challenged by the greater use of remote work. They typically have fewer resources and more limited access to funding to invest in the necessary technological and organisational changes. In contexts where access to broadband connection and online public services are more limited, SMEs suffer a greater competitive disadvantage than large firms. This can justify the deployment of different policy tools to support SMEs in their transition towards a hybrid working environment, where in-presence and remote work can coexist at the firm, team or individual level.

While it is too early to evaluate if any of the public policy instruments countries deployed in 2020-21 yielded the expected return, a synthesis of the main areas of intervention is possible. Relevant practices include setting up online platforms for remote work and other digital services; providing information and training on remote work opportunities and challenges for SMEs; enabling access to remote professional training for SMEs; and providing financial support for SMEs to take up remote working practices (OECD, 2020[42]). If many programmes supported SMEs' investment in IT hardware and software, fewer provided funds for complementary expenses such as consulting or training for entrepreneurs and workers to deal with remote working. One such case was the inclusion of telework among the refundable expenses in the **Industria**

Digitala 2021 initiative (Basque Country, **Spain**). The programme subsidises between 25% (large firms) and 50% (micro and small-sized firms) of the expenditure incurred for the acquisition of technology but also digital skills and diagnosis and implementation support. Other initiatives are non-financial in nature instead, and help spread information on existing best practices for the uptake of remote work. One recent example is **Flanders' Telewerk Action Plan**, which has guided workers and firms during the pandemic and aims to make this model a sustainable part of the future of work.

Box 3.7. Telewerk Action Plan – Flanders, Belgium

In the Telewerk Action Plan, the Flemish Government gathers a number of initiatives aimed to facilitate firms' and workers' transitions towards remote work, with a special focus on SMEs. The key aspects include:

- A web portal (within "Werkbaar werk") that collects information on remote work, including the legal framework, available financial support measures, guidelines for managers, webinars, self-assessment tools and a number of successful case studies.
- "Workability vouchers" ("Werkbaarheidscheques") that reduce firm's cost of professional advice on how to best organise remote work and reduce workers' psychological cost of the transition.
- The appointment of an inter-sectoral advisor who is tasked to map out the needs for remote work in the various sectors.
- A monthly monitor of teleworking adoption, via enterprise surveys.
- Links to the career guidance services offered by the Flemish Service for Employment and Vocational Training (VDAB), and to ESF-funded initiatives aimed at developing digital skills and other skills for remote working (e.g. leadership and communication skills).
- A consulting and co-ordinating effort about remote work policies between regional and federal authorities.

3.3. Fostering management and leadership skills

The success of these measures is not exclusively linked to the provision of services or expertise on these specific aspects, but depends in an important way on the leadership of managers and owners, as they ultimately decide on change and skills strategies within the firm. Ensuring their commitment to investment in human capital is therefore a key prerequisite for making adult learning a reality in smaller firms (OECD, 2020[40]; OECD, 2019[1]).

The linkages between management practices and firm productivity has been broadly documented in the academic literature and supported by an increasing number of country specific and cross-country firm surveys. As an example, the World Management Survey, which is conducted since 2004 in more than 30 countries, shows that management practices account for around 30% of total factor productivity (TFP) in the manufacturing sector, both across and within countries (Bloom, Sadun and Van Reenen, 2016[43]). In several instances, family ownership compounds the problem: managerial quality is lower in firms which are fully managed by the owning family (Bloom, Sadun and Van Reenen, 2016[43]), and family management is negatively associated to firm performance, on average across country (Bloom and Van Reenen, 2007[44]). While good managerial practices and skilled managers are two distinct aspects of firms' managerial capabilities, the association of good managerial practices to firm productivity is largely explained by the human capital of managers (Bender et al., 2018[45]).Improving management practices requires changes in both the supply of and the demand for managers.

Measures that aim to foster management and leadership skills are therefore important to promote investment in human capital for the competitiveness and productivity of the company. A recent OECD comparative analysis of government programmes aimed at improving managerial skills in small enterprises, mostly from traditional sectors of the economy (e.g. retail trade and low-tech manufacturing), finds that combining management training and consulting with support in ICT use is a common approach to boosting innovation in small low-tech enterprises (OECD, 2016[30]; Marchese et al., 2019[46]).

These measures all envisage a highly tailored approach: by culture (every entrepreneur feels its company is a world apart from all others) or as a consequence of the realities of production, business leaders prefer training that is highly specific to their territory, sector and ultimately company. This requires a set of training instruments that emphasises such tailored and often personalised approach: vouchers, coaching, mentoring. Moreover, good support practices follow the (digitalisation, internationalisation, or reskilling) project throughout at least part of its life. Indeed an initial assistance on the design of the project does not exclude that serious implementation difficulties can emerge along the project's life, and make the initial support irrelevant.

Owner-managers of small firms are found to generally prefer mentoring and longer-term business development programmes with intensive training and support sessions at intervals (Stone, 2010[16]). Measures adopted across European countries indeed tend to favour **mentoring, peer learning and coaching**, with the aim to build general leadership and management skills, or to focus on specific aspects such as building skills linked to the digital transformation and management of change. By fostering trust between instructors and learners, and leveraging the value of peers' experience, coaching and mentoring are especially valuable for those business leaders who do not think any intervention is needed. Successful coaching and mentoring happen in small groups (or even solely between the instructor and the business leader), and they require the active involvement of the trainee.

Providing public support to SMEs by introducing an external consultant or coach is important because firms, and especially SMEs, often lack a strategic and long-term vision and are not fully aware of their needs in terms of technology, business planning, organisation or investment in their workforce. Even if aware of their needs, SMEs more than large firms lack the financial resources to cover the cost of consultants or coaches as offered by private consulting companies. The concrete support given by the coach or a consultant to the SME has proven successful. Coaching in particular helps CEOs or owners gain a longer term vision, develop a positive attitude towards risk, engage in restructuring, and increase motivation among the staff (OECD, 2017[47]).

Evidence from existing practices suggests that coaching, mentoring and peer learning have overall a positive impact. Companies where coaching or mentoring takes place benefit from sharing and acquiring knowledge of best leadership and management practices, as well as from the creation and establishment of new networks and contacts. This type of measure seems particularly suitable for SMEs, as their sensitivity to extra costs for long-term investment, average lower margins and lower ability to raise funds increase the return to information sharing from other businesses.

Mentoring is widely employed in Ireland and the United Kingdom. SMEs in **Ireland** have good access to mentoring opportunities, which are offered by the main public providers of business and training support and services. Management development training and leadership development programmes are also available in Ireland through **Skillnet**, the business support agency of the Government of Ireland that supports businesses in their skills needs, and Enterprise Ireland (see also Box 4.1 in the next chapter).

Box 3.8. Mentoring in Ireland

Mentoring is widely employed in the Irish business advisory services system. The main public providers of mentoring services are the local enterprise offices, Enterprise Ireland (EI) and Skillnet Ireland, InterTradeIreland (the agency supporting internationalisation of SMEs in Ireland and Northern Ireland), but sectoral actors, incubators and accelerators are also involved in the provision of mentoring services.

Beyond internal advisors, Enterprise Ireland offers SMEs companies and High Potential Start Ups (HPSUs) access to a wide network of experts in Ireland and overseas, connecting companies with strategic advice and knowledge that can support them in addressing business challenges, and developing and executing growth strategies. Enterprise Ireland maintains a Mentor Network, a network of more than 400 highly experienced business people, who can offer advice and guidance, on a one to one basis. This network is shared with Local Enterprise Offices, which also have a panel of local mentors, used for referrals for their start-ups and micro-enterprise clients.

Mentors of the EI Mentor Network do not act as consultants, but offer advice based on their business experience. Companies can apply for a mentor through development advisors within EI, which then matches the company with a short list of mentors from which to choose. The mentorship is face-to-face and is based on an agreement and mutual understanding of the objectives and goals to be achieved. Depending on the needs, the duration of the mentorship can last 3, 6 or 12 months. Enterprise Ireland provides grant support to qualifying companies towards the cost of a mentor for up to 10 sessions (to a total of EUR 1 750). This amount is paid directly to the mentor, not as a fee, but as a per diem to secure their commitment. Mentors' profiles are reviewed on an individual basis by EI, on the basis of the needs of the client base and after a monthly recruitment day. All Mentors sign a confidentiality agreement with Enterprise Ireland.

In addition to one-on-one mentorships, EI organises mentors panels where companies in the early stages of development can present and gain feedback on their business plans and investment proposals. It also offers half-day deep-dive advisory sessions on different challenges that businesses can normally encounter and International Advisory Panels. The Panels are groups of senior private sector executives, who volunteer to advise CEOs and senior managers of Irish companies targeting international markets. While guidance is provided to mentors upon acceding the network, a recent evaluation has noted that considering the widespread use of mentoring in the Irish system, there could be space for a review of training and guidelines provided to mentors who are publicly funded, to assess the current situation and potentially consider strengthening the process of orientation, training and certification of these figures.

Source: Indecon (2019[48]), *Evaluation of Skillnet Ireland in 2018;* Enterprise Ireland (2020[49]), *How to Become an Enterprise Ireland Business Mentor.*

In the **United Kingdom**, the **Small Business Leadership Programme** (2018) is part of a package of measures to assist businesses in improving their productivity. The programme is a fully funded 10-week management training programme delivered by a consortium of business schools. Targeted at SMEs, aims to reach 10 000 beneficiaries by 2025. It is accompanied by other measures, aimed at strengthening local networks focused on business improvement, and at getting UK's leading businesses signed-up to mentoring programmes (OECD, 2020[19]). SMEs' leaders are in fact further supported through **Peer Networks**, a programme that brings together diverse cohorts of business leaders through high-impact group discussions and sessions, and by **Be The Business**, an independent charity with a large business network, which strongly leverages on practice and knowledge sharing and mentoring. The charity has been funded to help SMEs better understand how their productivity levels can be increased by best practice leadership and management techniques and making use of tried and tested technologies.

Box 3.9. Mentoring and peer learning in the United Kingdom

Peer Network is a programme aimed at SMEs aimed to support their leaders through peer learning and high impact group sessions, where they gain and reflect on feedback from their peers and identify practical solutions to overcome challenges of their business. Guided by expert facilitators, SMEs leaders are supported to create a trusted support network, helping to build and strengthen their business. The programme works through free, online group sessions moderated by a facilitator and/or delivered locally by Growth Hubs. The programme targets SMEs with at least five employees and GBP 100 000 turnover.

Be the Business is an independent charity gathering large and small businesses, which want to improve their performance and share their experiences to help others do the same. It provides inspiration, practical tools and free resources for businesses to identify opportunities for improvement and develop approaches that can boost their productivity. Its main working tools are expert analysis and advice from the business community, transmitted through mentoring programmes and peer learning groups. The charity is set to receive GBP 18.6 million of government funding to support SMEs in the adoption of best practice leadership and management techniques.

Source: Gov.UK (2020[50]), *Small business support schemes: Small Business Leadership Programme and Peer Networks*; Be the Business (2020[51]), https://www.bethebusiness.com/.

In **Italy**, the Turin Chamber of commerce runs a mentoring programme that encourages the exchange of managerial experiences across international markets between entrepreneurs.

Box 3.10. Mentoring by the Turin Chamber of Commerce – Italy

The Turin Chamber of commerce runs a mentoring programme that encourages the exchange of managerial experiences across international markets with business leaders with personal or professional ties to the Piedmont region. The programme consists in a voluntary relationship between a business professional with well-recognised work experience (mentor) and a new entrepreneur (mentee), where the mentor facilitates the professional development of his/her mentees. The programme is open to business owners as well as to high-ranked managerial positions.

Mentors are Italian professionals living abroad, with ties with Piedmont by origin, study or work and must have more than 10 years of proved experience in the field of management and business development. Mentees are mostly company executives or managers of companies based in Piedmont that work towards the international growth of their company.

Both parties engage in the relationship on a voluntary, non-paid basis within ethical guidelines. The Mentoring lasts at least 8 months with the aim to improve the internationalisation process of the companies and sharing good practice experiences. The project starts with a kick off meeting, in person, with mentors meeting potential mentees, facilitating the right matching.

Mentors and mentees interested in the programme has rapidly increased, with applicants going from 76 (1st edition) to 130 (3rd edition). 90% of the applicants are satisfied with the Programme, gaining new strategic plans to grow internationally, new marketing and communication strategies, business plans, organisational changes, development of international contacts. The programme has the potential to help mentees enter a new international market and acquire new contacts and networks.

The main reported challenges are linked to finding the right matches and ensuring that the mentoring relationship is not interrupted.

The Mentoring programme is easily replicable in other regions, as it is mainly based on the networking capabilities of the Chamber of Commerce, both through the mentors and the mentees. The programme is funded through the ERDF.

Source: *Interreg* database of good practices.

In Sweden, peer learning and coaching of key representatives within SMEs has been used with specific focus on digitalisation, with the aim to build the capacity of SMEs with regard to digital transformation. The **Kickstart Digitalisering (Kickstart Digitalisation)** and **INDIGO** are both part of Sweden's Smart Industry Strategy, and leverage on peer learning and mentoring in order to provide companies with inspiring examples and in-depth knowledge, help them identify opportunities and adopt digital technologies.

These programmes have received positive participant feedback and proved successful in affecting digital maturity of SMEs and strengthening networks of companies and institutions. Using co-operative coaching and learning sessions that can take into consideration the context of participating firms was especially considered a positive element (Ramboll, 2018[52]). In addition, it was made evident that SMEs need continuous and operational support when it comes to implementing solutions, making coaching a useful tool to aid to companies overcome challenges during the implementation of new digital solutions (Tillväxtverket, 2020[53]).

Box 3.11. Kickstart Digitalisering and coaching – Sweden

The **Kickstart initiative** is a national initiative in which small and medium-sized Swedish businesses attend workshops to inspire them to begin their own digitalisation effort.

The programme seeks to de-dramatise digitalisation, showing that it concerns all companies and thus lowering the entry or initial investment cost for firms. It enables peer-learning between the participating companies and provides good examples of digitalisation. The initiative is indeed based on a participatory design that brings together actors at different levels, through a series of workshops over a six-week period, consisting of three free-of-charge meetings where two representatives from approximately ten companies share experiences and ideas.

The programme has been carried out by the Association of Swedish Engineering Industries, RISE Research Institutes of Sweden, IF Metall, IUC and Swedish Incubators & Science Parks (SISP), and has been financed by The Swedish Agency for Economic and Regional Growth. A total of 627 companies participated in 75 "kickstarts", which means that the goal was achieved with good margin. 75% of the participants the companies had 50 or fewer employees and 70% were manufacturing companies, the remainder operating in the service sector. After the project, a large share of these companies started a digitalisation project or increased the pace of ongoing investment in digital technologies. Companies were satisfied with Kickstart as a concept, which has also been exported to Estonia, Latvia and Lithuania.

The result required amendments to the initial design of the programme. The initial goal or reaching 1 000 companies and 100 "kickstarts" was revised down, since it showed little capacity to scale after the pilot of 2016 to national dissemination. A major challenge was to reach companies and entice them to participate, as companies have limited resources and perceive digitalisation as an abstract phenomenon. A mitigation strategy adapted the programme's communication to focus on companies' needs and solutions, rather than digitalisation per se, showing clear examples of benefits.

Overall, Kickstart has contributed to a deeper understanding of digitalisation in companies. Another positive result of the project was the strengthening of networks between companies and between the company and the promotion actors. On the downside, companies proved to need continuous support in their digitalisation work to move forward, which is why the project has been expanded in 2020 to include coaching as a way to aid SMEs overcome capacity shortages in the implementation phase.

The Swedish Agency for Economic and Regional Growth has granted funding for coaching on digitalisation to several companies. These projects have mostly been conducted by local and regional parties, with a majority of them, implemented by regional chapters of IUC – a business-owned national network that aims to support Swedish business staying competitive, through their concept INDIGO.

The **INDIGO projects** provide companies with in-depth knowledge on digitalisation It offers a training programme that combines network meetings and joint workshops with coaching for the individual company, with a coach/consultant who supports concrete digitalisation efforts at the company, helping them to define needs and opportunities and to lay the foundation for a development strategy. As a rule, the coaching model involved a start-up meeting with management team/managers, coaching for 20-80 hours, knowledge seminars, follow-up meetings and an identification of the next steps. Participating companies are met at the early stages of their projects and are offered tailored advice, following an in-depth analysis of the company's situation and strategic development goals. Flexibility, low access thresholds and concrete objectives were important to ensure SMEs participation.

Source: Tillväxtverket (2020[53]), *Kickstart Digitalisering: Method.*

Similarly, in **Denmark**, **Scale-Up Denmark**, an accelerator programme that targets promising businesses and start-ups with a focus on smart specialisation, uses intensive development courses, peer learning, mentoring, workshops, access to venture capital and expertise, with the aim to create a group of high growth companies in the country. The programme has been funded through the European Regional Development Fund (ERDF), in addition to funds from the Danish regions, the Danish Business Authority and companies participating.

Box 3.12. Scale-up Denmark

Scale-up Denmark is a training concept that targets promising entrepreneurs and start-ups with the aim to establish an elite group of high-growth companies. While the country has a long history when it comes to developing entrepreneurial competences and supporting entrepreneurial learning and start-ups, creating scale-ups and high-growth company was considered a strategically important step for the Danish industry competitiveness.

Scale-up Denmark is an accelerator programme that targets the most promising national and international entrepreneurs within the business areas of the Danish regional smart specialisation strategy, through intensive development courses, professional discussions, mentoring, workshops and access to expert knowledge and venture capital. Large companies participate as partners of the initiative, thus allowing for a transfer of knowledge to young firms.

It is a four-year initiative, inspired by a private accelerator programme (Next Step Challenge) and funded by the ERDF, regions' own development funds, the Danish Business Authority and the participating companies, with total budget of EUR 22 million. The initiative is expected to identify 355 companies that will create 1 200 new jobs and an increase in turnover of EUR 266 million.

While the impact of the initiative is yet to be determined, it is an interesting example, which builds upon the positive experience of the Next Step challenge. As the precursor mostly attracted foreign participants, it is expected that Scale-up Denmark will find it challenging to attract Danish entrepreneurs.

Source: https://scale-updenmark.com.

4 Fostering entrepreneurial ecosystems

Networks and partnerships can help address the complex skills needs of SMEs, while addressing some of the challenges these companies face. Co-operation allows for pooling of resources, information sharing, knowledge exchange, developing ideas and learning from each other's experiences. In addition, promoting participatory approaches that involve of SMEs in the development, implementation and evaluation of measures that target investment in skills builds ownership and enhances learning within the companies.

4.1. Pooling of resources and SMEs participation

Pooling of resources can help address various obstacles to training confronting individual small firms. Among the different modalities of SME participation in firm partnerships, *learning and training networks* are prominent. Evidence suggests that developing networks can strengthen the engagement of small firms in training, developing the training itself, exchanging knowledge more broadly (Stone, 2010[16]). It can provide a solution for the complex needs for training of SMEs, as it allows for economies of scale and for the creation of a critical mass in the demand for education and training, including the analysis of skill gaps, thus lowering the per-worker cost of training.

Networks may involve local or sectoral co-operation among SMEs themselves, or between larger firms and their supply chain partners, including small firms. There can be a lead company responsible to provide the main service, or a consortium of equal partners.

While many networks are local in nature, others can formalise a collaboration that goes beyond the territorial dimension and the industrial specialisation. This is useful especially for territories that cannot supply certain advanced technologies that are needed for firms to thrive in the 21st century. Supply-chain relationships, however, remain an important and frequent component of networks. Indeed firms in a supply-chain relationship tend to purse the same goals, which counterbalances the natural forces of market competition and the "do-it-by-yourself" entrepreneurial culture characterising many SMEs. Successful networks therefore ask for a common, long-term vision. More short-lived, typically horizontal networks can also succeed, if they typically carry out a well-defined and time-bound project.

Policy makers can support firm networks by allowing these entities to apply for support alongside individual firms. Moreover, they can earmark specific resources for firm networks only. Public support can also differentiate rate of subsidisation for different objectives pursued by the network, including giving priority to up- and re-skilling initiatives. Many of the programmes presented above allow for the realisation of projects by individual companies or consortia/groups of employers. This is the case for example of the **Finnish Joint Purchasing Training Programme**, a scheme for subsidised training which supports employers – either individually or in groups – in the creation of training offers for their employees. Similarly, programmes such as **MKB!dee** in the Netherlands allow for the submission of project proposals by a partnership, which must include at least a certain minimum participation of SMEs.

Programmes can also have co-operation among companies, and especially on SMEs, as a specific focus. This is the case of the **Impulse Training Networks (Implus-Qualifizierungs-Verbund)** in Austria. They are networks through which companies can co-operate to provide cost-efficient and work-relevant training, organising and purchasing relevant qualifications for their employees. This is a long-standing subsidised programme, which is managed by the PES at national level and at the state level through a number of consulting companies, which provide support services to the networks for a maximum of ten consultation days. These services include setting up the network and its working processes or structures, as well as supporting the network in surveying the educational needs of its workforce and developing training plans and applications for available financial support for training. The acquisition of qualifications increases the potential of employees and keeps teams up-to-date and motivated.

This is a longstanding subsidy programme, which has been funded partly with ESF funds under programming periods 2007-13 and 2014-20, and is considered a key scheme to promote adult learning and joint training within SMEs in Austria (Cedefop, 2020[54]).

Box 4.1. Impulse Training Networks in Austria

Impulse Training Networks are an Austrian programme through which companies can co-operate to provide cost-efficient and work-relevant training. An "impulse qualification network" is a network of several companies jointly organising and purchasing promising training that delivers a qualification for the companies' employees. The programme is a key scheme to promote join training and learning in SMEs in Austria, and entered into force in 2007.

The PES fully funds support services for the running of these networks, including in the set-up of the networks, the development of training plans and development programmes and the application for available financial support for in-company training. The implementation is led by the PES at federal level and at state level commissioned to consulting companies that support the network companies with a maximum of ten consultation days covered. The tasks of the consulting companies include: the application, processing and billing of funding; help in structuring and defining processes within the network, including with regard to work organisations, roles, objectives and services offered; development of personnel development programmes; implementing a survey of skill needs; creating the curricula; researching and organising joint courses; co-ordinating activities. The network can also serve as a platform for information exchange and joint development projects and as an additional labour market policy offer for regional economic communities, business and industrial areas or business incubators.

In addition, the PES offers a subsidy that covers 50% of the costs of training of underserved groups (older and low skilled workers). Networks must be made up of at least three companies and 50% of companies in the network are required to be SMEs.

Source: AMS Arbeitsmarktservice (2020[55]), *Impuls-Qualifizierungsverbund*.

In Ireland, training networks are promoted by **Skillnet**, the business support agency that promotes and facilitates continuous learning in the country, with an approach that mixes sectoral and regional aggregation of firms into networks. The agency complements traditional training programmes with tailored training for groups of firms through its main programmes: the **Training Networks Programme**, which has supported 15 000 companies over 50 enterprise groups and 66 learning networks; and the **Future Skills Programme**, which provides seed funding for enterprise groups to develop innovative enterprise-led trainings with HEIs and private training providers.

Under the TNP Programme, networks funded need to conduct skill assessment of their members and promote subsidised training programmes, which can best respond to them, with exclusion of training which is mandatory by law which cannot be covered under the programme.

The work of the agency has had a proven effective to incentivise SMEs investment in skills, and increase participation in training (European Commission, 2020[24]).

Box 4.2. SkillNet – Private-public co-operation through learning networks in Ireland

Skillnet Ireland is an enterprise-led agency that promotes and facilitates continuous learning in Ireland with the objective to increase learning participation in enterprises. It is considered a successful public-private co-operation initiative and a good practice example internationally.

The agency supports learning networks representing specific sectors or regions with the aim to increase participation in enterprise training by companies, improve competitiveness and provide improved access for workers to industry-specific/transferable skills development. Its Flagship Training Networks Programme (TNP) supports enterprise-led learning and development, and skills supply responses. It does this through 65 learning networks.

The TNP is aimed at supporting training measures undertaken by enterprises with the purpose of developing and updating the knowledge of their workforce. Activities are organised in four pillars: partnerships to encourage training participation at sector level; growing the skills base by giving workers access to lifelong learning opportunities; developing local learning responses; building training in enterprises by continuously identifying and promoting best practice and quality in all aspects of the design, delivery, evaluation and dissemination of enterprise training.

Skillnet Ireland operates a joint investment model, where government funding of on-the-job training is matched by contributions from businesses. The allocation of funding is based on specific calls for proposals. Proposals are made by the networks.

Networks are furthermore required to conduct a Learning Needs Assessment of their member enterprises to gather information about their skill development requirements. Training which is mandatory under Irish law (e.g. health and safety training) does not receive funding under the TNP. To access the subsidised training, the company must become a member company of a network.

In 2018, the networks delivered over EUR 36 million worth of education and training programmes to more than 56 000 individuals in Ireland. Currently, Skillnet Ireland has close to 16 500 member companies, 95% of which are small and medium-sized enterprises and 56% are micro-enterprises with less than 10 employees. Evaluations of Skillnet Ireland show that companies perceive the training provided to be in line with labour market needs (Indecon, 2019[48]).

A key overall indicator of Skillnet Ireland's success has been the growth of its enterprise participation base across the organisation's networks. It achieved a growth of 9.7% on the number of enterprises between 2017 and 2018, and a 28% growth between 2015 and 2018. The organisation's SMEs represent approximately 5.2% of the overall population of SMEs in Ireland. In addition, new networks cover a diversity of sectors and skill needs, including robotics and automation technologies, micro- and nano-technologies, the recruitment and hospitality sectors, among others.

Source: Indecon (2019[48]), *Evaluation of Skillnet Ireland in 2018*; Skillnet Ireland (2020[56]) https://www.skillnetireland.ie/.

4.2. Leveraging ecosystems for skills investment

Co-operation between industry, institutions and academia encompass a large set of knowledge-transfer channels, such as collaborative research, co-patenting, or academic spinoffs. These interactions are the object of a vast literature (OECD, 2019[57]; Kreiling and Paunov, 2021[58]; OECD/European Union, 2019[59]), and fall largely outside the scope of the present study. Some forms of collaboration, however, also provide incentives to firms to expand their investment in human capital, e.g. via the hiring of R&D personnel, the development of new lines of production that require a more skilled workforce, or the design of education curricula that minimise the occurrence of skill mismatches in the labour market. If industry-university co-operation reduces the cost of a firm's access to high-skilled workforce, then SMEs are poised to benefit from these initiatives more than firms that can leverage economies of scale. In this context, various programmes and policy strategies have been used to ensure partnerships that involve stakeholders from all relevant sectors.

Entrepreneurial and innovative ecosystems[4] in particular have been largely promoted in European countries with the aim to foster co-operation among different actors, including entrepreneurial actors and organisations, as well as institutions including academia.

The European Commission recently produced a roadmap with clear strategic steps that need to be taken at European and national level to ensure that SMEs access talent relevant to their digitalisation journey, identifying the importance of ecosystems in this regard. In particular, according to the roadmap, ecosystems should be strengthened and strong leadership activated within these environments, as to promote strategies and best practices and increased awareness within SMEs.

Inspiring examples of different measures and initiatives that strengthen ecosystems and facilitate their development are present in different countries, with specific measures aimed at building SMEs capacity and knowledge, when it comes to digital transformation and digital competences. Competence centres are example of ecosystems that do so.

In **Germany**, the **Mittelstand 4.0-Kompetenzzentren, SME 4.0 Competence Centres** are part of the German policy for SMEs on Industry 4.0 – Mittelstand 4.0 already presented above. They are cross-sector and cross-thematic digitalisation ecosystems supporting knowledge and technology transfer to SMEs. They combine subsidised training and other forms of financial support with free capacity building activities for SMEs on the topic of digitalisation. On the information side, they present firms with concrete actions and solutions in relation to skill development.

Box 4.3. Mittelstand 4.0-Kompetenzzentren – Germany

The Mittelstand 4.0 Competence Centres are meant to be cross-sector and cross-thematic digitalisation ecosystems supporting the knowledge and technology transfer to SMEs. By offering workshops, demonstration plants and networks with representatives of the complete value chain, SMEs are practically supported in developing their own Industry 4.0 solutions.

The Centres' work does not favour any particular provider and is available free of charge. SMEs are free to access the centres directly and receive consultations and advices for free. Since 2015, the Economic Affairs Ministry has set up a total of 26 Mittelstand 4.0 centres that provide the Mittelstand (SMEs) with information and support about digitisation. A combination of regional centres in all parts of Germany and specific thematic centres delivers a wide range of support for all sorts of sectors and corporate needs. Workshops, training sessions, practical tests, webinars and interventions, designed with SMEs in mind.

The projects within Mittelstand-Digital are completely funded by the BMWi. The BMWi issues an invitation to tender to which project consortia can apply for. The project consortium describes in detail their action plan to achieve the objectives of the tender. Although the Mittelstand 4.0 Competence Centres are funded by the BMWi, a separate project management agency oversees all Mittelstand 4.0 Competence Centres.

The Mittelstand 4.0 competence centres reached around 60 000 companies at over 100 locations in 2018, with a network of over 800 experts, 18 regional and 8 thematic competence centres.

Source: BMWi (2019[60]), *SMEs Digital – Strategies for the digital transformation.*

Similarly, in **Austria, Competence Centres for Excellent Technologies (COMET)** are in place since 2006 and their current rationale is to develop new expertise and encourage greater internationalisation, as a sign of excellent co-operative research. Recently they have also supported numerous projects that link digitalisation and circular economy.

Box 4.4. Austrian Competence Centres for Excellent Technologies (COMET)

Austrian Competence Centres for Excellent Technologies (COMET) were launched in 2006 and are internationally recognised as best practice. They develop new expertise and encourage greater internationalisation as a sign of excellent co-operative research. Defining promising fields of research via science-industry collaboration creates new ideas, encourage technology transfer, and strengthen the innovative capacity of companies. Their objectives are:

- Developing skills through long-term research co-operation between science and industry at the highest level;
- Strengthening Austria as a research location;
- Strengthening the competitiveness of science and industry by driving internationalisation as a sign of high quality co-operative research: involving internationally-renowned scientists, organisations and companies, positioning COMET Centres as internationally attractive partners, and benchmarking with top research institutions;
- Establishing and developing human resources: increasingly attracting scientists of international renown, creating structured career models for scientists, and actively supporting inter-sectoral mobility for research personnel in order to intensify the transfer of know-how.

COMET are managed by the Austrian Research Promotion Agency (FFG) on behalf of the Federal Ministry for Climate Action, Environment, Energy, Mobility, Innovation and Technology (BMK) and the Federal Ministry for Digital and Economic Affairs (BMDW). The Austrian provinces support COMET with additional funds. Evaluations showed that COMET increase the expertise and innovative output of the companies involved, help consolidate existing research areas and scientific expertise.

Several supported centres and projects develop expertise in the circular economy. For instance, the COMET Competence Centre for Recycling and Recovery of Waste 4.0 (ReWaste 4.0) promotes waste management and new Industry 4.0 approaches based on digital networking and robotics technology (European Commission, 2020[7]).

Source: European Commission (2020[7]), *Skills for SMEs – Cybersecurity, Internet of Things and Big Data for Small and Medium-Sized Enterprises;* FFG (2020[61]), https://www.ffg.at/en/comet/programme.

In **Denmark**, a bottom-up and industry-science co-operation initiative developed since 2014. **MADE** – the Manufacturing Academy of Denmark – implements collaborative actions, which promote productivity through applied research, innovation and education. It constitutes an inspiring example of bottom-up initiative, which is quickly developing an innovation ecosystem in the Danish manufacturing sector. Since 2017, **MADE Digital** aims to develop a Danish approach to Industry 4.0 with a focus on its SMEs.

MADE Digital was launched as a collaboration project to enable scientists and practitioners from companies to work together and implement digital solutions, tailor-made to the specific needs of Danish manufacturing companies. Within this initiative, large companies collaborate with smaller companies, research teams from universities and technical experts from the regional training organisations on topics linked to digitalisation. Their aim is to provide industry with new knowledge and help SMEs implement digital solutions, particularly assess which services within the firm could gain most from digitalisation. (Larosse, 2017[62])

Being mostly funded by business sector contributions and the Danish Innovation Fund, this project enables strong and co-ordinated digital development especially for SMEs, which can gain knowledge of the latest technological possibilities. The programme is similar to the Industry 4.0 programmes developed in Germany, but it has been tailored to the Danish context, where leading companies are non-competitors, building on diversity and enabling co-operation among them (Larosse, 2017[62]).

In the **Netherlands**, **Katapult** is a learning network of more than 300 industry-education partnerships that is showing positive results in bringing together education, business and society. The network combines relevant knowledge about collaboration, support to public-private partnerships with free tools and guidance, including individual support from experts through all phases of the collaboration. Different instruments proposed include knowledge sharing, workshop and lessons, study visit to other inspiring partnerships, research within SMEs by university or VET students and learning events. Importantly, online tools are available and open source for stakeholders to access.

Box 4.5. MADE-Digital – Denmark

MADE – Manufacturing Academy of Denmark is the Danish innovation and research platform for the manufacturing industry in Denmark. The initiative started in 2014 as a bottom-up initiative for industry-science co-operation and it is implementing collaborative actions under the second area of the proposed Digital Growth agenda (Attractive digital growth environment), to promote production in Denmark through applied industrial research, innovation and education, enabling increase in productivity and growth. MADE achieves its goals through the development of strategic partnerships between industry and academia.

MADE has two main programmes where industry and academic partners are working together:

- MADE SPIR (Strategic Platform for Innovation and Research), which aims to develop Advanced Manufacturing technologies and strengthen the Danish manufacturing ecosystem (suppliers, end user companies, research and education)
- MADE Digital is a research and innovation platform aimed at developing a Danish approach to Industry 4.0, where there is focus on the many Danish SMEs.

MADE Digital builds on the research of MADE SPIR with the aim of accelerating the digital transformation of Danish manufacturing companies.

In MADE Digital, large companies collaborate with smaller companies, research teams from universities and technical experts from the regional training organisations. The research themes are distributed along nine areas: Smart industrial products; Digital assistance tools; Sensor technologies and production data; Digital manufacturing process; Smart factories; Intelligent supply chains; Organising digital production; Automation with collaborative robots; Digital design.

The aim of the project is to provide new knowledge through research and help large-scale companies and SMEs to implement digital solutions. Particularly SMEs will be helped to assess which part of the factory or which service within the company will gain most from digitalisation.

Today MADE is run as a non-profit association, and the members of MADE are Danish companies, research and knowledge institutions and organisations. Approximately two-thirds of business members are SMEs. The members of MADE are each year charged a membership fee, depending on the type of organisation and number of employees. Members of MADE have then free access to activities, events and services. About 50% of the funding comes from companies, 40% from the Danish Innovation Fund, and the remaining share from universities, private funds and associations.

Source: Larosse (2017[62]), *Analysis of national initiatives on digitising European Industry: Denmark*; MADE Digital (2020[63]), https://www.made.dk/digital/.

Partnerships within this network are considered generally successful, and the network has witnessed high growth. Today, it serves about 14 000 firms, with the goal to reach 20 000 companies by 2025 and to have a coverage of 90% of schools for senior vocational education, as well as of the Universities of Applied Sciences, participating to a centre's activities.

Box 4.6. Katapult – The Netherlands

Katapult is a network of more than 300 partnerships between education and business in the Netherlands. It gathers all public-private partnerships in the Netherlands, organises meetings, collects the relevant knowledge about collaborations, and offers individual support from experts. Its objective is to improve co-operation between the education sector, businesses and society.

This is done with a variety of measures, including business professionals providing lessons and students conducting research for an SME company during their studies. The network also organises a number of activities and meetings that bring together partnerships.

A set of tools is available to support partnerships throughout the five main phases of a project's life (start, development, expansion, maintenance, validation). Tools are open source and include:

- Model phase, to help determine which actions to take, based on the phase the firm's project is in;
- Impact study questionnaire: a tool used to make a scan of the firm's skills ecosystem and to measure the project's impact;
- An overview of the firm's partners;
- Various workshop tools to facilitate the discussion with partners;
- Benchmarks with other projects, and relevant best practices;
- Database of contracts and collaboration models;
- Peer review model.

This effective public-private collaboration quickly gained strong support after starting to bring together in an unique community the Centres of expertise (within higher education) and Centres for innovative craftsmanship (within vocational education), which promote collaboration between entrepreneurs, vocational schools, higher education institutions and government. The Centres were promoted by the Dutch Government, with the first pilots in 2011. Each centre is autonomous, has its own characteristics, and creates its niche and own market value. Shared investments of both public and private parties help drive business models that create financial viability. Through associations with education organisations, new insights, methods and curricula reach an extended audience (Cedefop, 2018[64]).

75% of the partnerships within Katapult are considered successful and the programme is already beyond the pilot phase and is scaling up. The Katapult network intends to increase outreach and sustainability and to explore and launch strategies to involve more regional stakeholders in the centres' activities. Within the first two years of operation, the number of involved businesses doubled (Cedefop, 2018[64]). Katapult is actively working to increase the number of SMEs within partnerships and their effectiveness within them, registering overall increased interest within small businesses.

Source: CEDEFOP (2018[64]), the Netherlands*: public-private partnerships will promote innovation in VET*; Katapult (2020[65]), https://wearekatapult.eu/.

4.3. Making information available and easy to access

A last set of measures promote information access and ease of understanding on support services available to companies and are therefore instrumental in incentivising SMEs access and participation in skill-enhancing initiatives (OECD, 2020[19]).

Some of the measures presented above, such as competence centres, already contribute to this goal. In other cases governments design and finance awareness campaigns, such as the Irish **Supporting SMEs** campaign. The 12-month campaign developed an online guide ("Supporting SMEs Online Tool") that helped Irish start-ups and small businesses navigate the range of 80 public support policies dedicated to them and find the one that best fits with their specific needs. The training levy scheme (i.e. Skillnet Ireland) is one of these instruments. Business leaders and representatives play a key role in promoting the campaign.

Other good practices develop virtual one-stop-shops (*portals*) that provide information for companies on existing opportunities for funding and support, as well as information on good examples from previous applications in other companies.

Portals of this type exist in different countries with different aims and content. In Sweden, for example, the Agency for Economic and Regional Growth has developed a search service called **Digitise your Company,** which aims to help companies find offers that can stimulate digitalisation in SMEs, while funding from the Agency has been used by a research institute (RISE) to create a knowledge bank on digitalisation for companies **Time to Digitise**. The agencies disseminated and lobbied for the use of the portals during seminars and lectures, company meetings and individual meetings.

A more encompassing analysis of European good practices reveals a few common features of success. A key role is played by employers' associations and Chambers of Commerce, and, to a lesser extent, by trusted professionals (e.g. tax accountants, employment consultants) that already know the company which is interested in touching the support. Indeed a direct contact with the entrepreneur has proven to be most effective. Furthermore, dissemination campaign should rely on "accessible" and time-saving instruments such as online "how-to" guidelines, short webinars, and transform into ad-hoc, tailor-made approaches in a second step, for firms that manifest their interest. Lastly, the participation of well-known figures in the entrepreneurial world increases the probability that the message is well-received by other business leaders.

Box 4.7. Making information and offerings easy to access – the Swedish case

Digitise your company is an online search service available at www.verksamt.se/digitalindustri and developed by the Swedish Agency for Economic and Regional Growth, as part of a larger portal offering services to companies. The purpose of the service is to help small businesses find current instruments that promote digitalisation in SMEs. The portal allows searches by the following areas: digitalisation, sustainable production, innovation and competence.

Similarly, RISE, the Swedish Research Institute, developed www.dagsattdigitalisera.se – Time to Digitise, a knowledge bank on digitalisation for companies. The platform was developed with funding from the Swedish Agency for Economic and Regional Growth, under the Digitalisation Promotion initiative. The purpose was to complement physical meetings of projects such as Kickstart Digitalisation with digital tools, so that companies got access to several opportunities to familiarise with what digitalisation can mean for their business. Time to digitise was published in the summer of 2019 and offers free and easily accessible content in 12 areas linked to digitalisation, with over 200 films that are divided in basic and in-depth parts. Of these movies, 20 specifically highlight how SMEs work with digitalisation. Time to Digitise was further supplemented during the autumn of 2019 with ten workshop concepts, where parts of the material were packaged to enable modular use.

Through Time to Digitise, SMEs get access to material they can use according to specific needs and have the possibility to download content and create ideas and action plans for further work. The portal has had more than 15 000 views and 6 500 users have used the tools on www.dagsattdigitalisera.se and 780 of them have created their own accounts to continue working. In addition, dissemination took place in seminars and lectures, in company contacts and in individual meetings.

5 Conclusions

Governments can provide incentives for firms to invest in skills in a variety of ways, thus addressing the misalignment between the supply and demand of skills and promoting the competitiveness and productivity of SMEs. This report provides an overview of a range of policy instruments available to governments that have proven effective among small and medium-sized enterprises in different countries.

In line with the good practice examples provided, the evidence suggests that a good and effective policy toolkit should include both financial and non-financial incentives, which lower the costs of investment and support SMEs in building or accessing the resources a needed to invest effectively in skills.

Subsidies seem to be the most suitable form of financial incentives when it comes to SMEs. Vouchers especially are among the most used incentives to support small businesses, with co-funding and cost sharing systems being the most common. These should be combined with effective support measures to help SMEs identify their skill needs, promote the most relevant forms of training for their workforce, and use the skills available to them in an effective way.

Good examples from European countries include Skill Assessment and Anticipation (SAA) services administered through external operators, such as the PES or consultants, or services which aim to build internal capacity through the promotion of modern HR systems, High Performance Working Practices and other forms of workplace innovation, as well as management capacity. Among this type of measures, diagnostic tools for self-assessment are an affordable way to help SMEs assess and identify their needs, as they can be easy to implement. Coaching, mentoring and peer learning are also broadly used and are suitable for SMEs, as they promote knowledge sharing and transfer, and build on concrete practices from successful entrepreneurs, especially when it comes to working with managers and company executives.

Co-operative coaching and learning sessions are especially effective in improving the take-up of digital technologies in SMEs, as each firms' history and context can be taken into account. However, as firms also require continuous and operational support for the implementation of solutions, measures that combine peer learning and individual support services, for example through subsidised consulting/coaching services, seem to be best placed to help SMEs invest in the key competences for the digital transformation.

Among measures aimed to foster co-operation among companies, learning and training networks have proven effective in promoting SMEs investment in human capital. Good examples include subsidies for the development of networks or for the training activities developed under the networks, as well as guidance on financial incentives available to cover costs of training, or direct expertise to develop skill assessments.

Similarly, competence centres and measures that help firms creating partnerships with public and education sectors can be successful in promoting inclusive skill ecosystems, as well as digitalisation ecosystems, thus supporting knowledge and technology transfer to SMEs, as well as promoting working-learning programmes strengthening SMEs.

Based on an analysis of the good practices presented in this study, a number of elements can be identified that are instrumental to the success of the different measures and interventions for promoting investment by SMEs in skills:

- Take-up and satisfaction are higher when the administrative burden is low, i.e. application and compliance procedures are easy, and when there is certainty of funding.
- Measures that factor in the indirect costs and opportunity costs of training, and that cover informal learning in addition to formal and non-formal training can facilitate skills investment by SMEs. The adoption in European countries of National Frameworks for Qualifications should contribute to this goal: the Framework should improve the transparency and comparability of qualifications of different regional systems and foster geographic and professional mobility. Further efforts could be made to integrate micro-credentials and learning acquired informally on the job in the framework, where not yet present.
- Co-funding or cost-sharing models are most common and effective. While this is already a common standard in several measures across OECD countries, special arrangements could be designed for the participation of SMEs, which cannot necessarily absorb the initial cost of setting up training for their workers.
- Programmes typically including a mix of hands-on consultancy and financial incentives. Bundling of financial and non-financial instruments is usually a good way to increase participation to the schemes and the return on the financial investment.
- Programmes and measures should respond to specific needs or challenges of individual companies, as SMEs often lack the capacity or resources to see how certain measures can be tailored to their specific context. Measures that include practice and knowledge sharing, as well as measures that can easily adapt to the needs of each company are for this reason most suitable for SMEs. Competence Centres, as e.g. in Austria and Germany, are shaping up to become an important venue for knowledge exchange, in particular with the higher education sector. Flexible programme delivery is also important in an environment with limited resources for investment, for example when requiring management involvement and in-person presence in workshops or training, or in terms of modular and distance provision of training and measures.
- Access to clear information is very important to foster the take up of support measures by SMEs. This can be achieved through close collaboration and open and proactive channels of communication between companies and the agencies managing the measures.
- SMEs do not often participate in networks of companies or with other stakeholders of the digital transformation, perhaps due to more limited information or trust in the network partners. Strategies to increase participation include awareness-raising activities, early and personal contact with companies, as well as the use and sharing of practical good practice examples from other companies.

Micro and small-sized firms in particular face additional challenges in investing in skills development and in introducing new technologies, compared to larger firms, calling for policy solutions that are targeted to their specific needs. The general principles described above apply even more so for micro and small-sized firms.

1. *Reduce the cost of compliance*

Many micro and small-sized firms do not make use of government support for adult learning activities because they lack the capacity (e.g. a dedicated HR department), financial resources, or time to apply for support and comply with the ensuing administrative requirements. Administrative costs for the beneficiaries (e.g. delays in reimbursements, multiple simultaneous applications, complex procedures, etc.) should be minimised. This could be done by providing micro and small-sized firms with tailored conditions in terms of generosity of the support, application procedures, or reimbursement practices (e.g. setting a first tranche of reimbursement as soon as possible to foster uptake from cash-constrained firms).

2. *Leverage informal learning*

As training in micro and small-sized firms is more frequently informal in nature, more tailored help may be required to help these firms recognise and validate informal learning. In addition, initiatives that cover the cost of labour for workers participating in training are potentially more interesting for micro and small-sized firms, where the opportunity cost of the hours dedicated to training is high.

3. *Identify flexible solutions*

Many micro and small-sized firms are mid- or low-tech companies, and require technological solutions that are relatively affordable, easy to implement, and often already in use in other firms operating in the same sector. To match this heterogeneity and maximise its returns, training in micro and small-sized firms should be flexible in content (e.g. tailored to the needs of the firm and covering both technical and soft skills), provision (e.g. modular training, distance training, training outside working hours) and recipients (e.g. involving the entrepreneur as well).

4. *Provide guidance to managers and entrepreneurs*

Managerial skills are often more limited in micro, small and family-led businesses than in large or publicly-owned companies. Training for managers contributes to raise awareness of the benefits of up- and re-skilling, and to better address skills gaps within companies. Existing skills assessment tools are considered useful, but more support should be given to managers in the interpretation of the results of the assessment, and in the identification of actionable and targeted solutions. Actions aimed at improving the learning culture and the use of public support instruments in micro and small-sized firms should further target the entrepreneurs or business owners, as they are usually the locus of control in the firm. This can be achieved via external expertise from people that the entrepreneur can trust, such as representatives from employers' associations, professionals (e.g. tax accountants, employment consultants), or other business leaders. Policy actions could also raise awareness of public policy instruments, or aim at improving the quality of the consulting expertise provided to SMEs.

5. *Foster collaboration*

Micro and small-sized firms have limited resources to formalise collaboration with other firms or other institutions that contribute to bolster their innovation capacity. A greater involvement of micro and small-sized firms in company networks or associations, as well as the development of joint strategies within the supply chains of larger companies would reduce training costs and promote the exchange of knowledge. Policy interventions should also target existing intermediary structures between the policy maker and firms in order to: raise awareness and the use of existing support instruments; accompany firms in their upskilling strategy; and involve firms in a broader network of institutions, including universities and other post-secondary education institutions. The collaborations can also supply skills that are not locally available, as is likely the case for the mastery of some new technologies or organisational practices.

References

AMS Arbeitsmarktservice (2020), *Impuls-Qualifizierungsverbund*, https://www.ams.at/unternehmen/personal--und-organisationsentwicklung/impuls-qualifizierungs-verbund-iqv. [55]

Anact-Aract (2018), *Expérimentation Afest - Action de Formation En Situation de Travail: Rapport Final.* [28]

Be the Business (2020), , https://www.bethebusiness.com/. [51]

Bender, S. et al. (2018), "Management practices, workforce selection, and productivity", *Journal of Labor Economics*, Vol. 36/S1, pp. S371-S409, http://dx.doi.org/10.1086/694107. [45]

Bloom, N., R. Sadun and J. Van Reenen (2016), *Management as a Technology?*, National Bureau of Economic Research, Cambridge, MA, http://dx.doi.org/10.3386/w22327. [43]

Bloom, N. and J. Van Reenen (2007), *Measuring and Explaining Management Practices Across Firms and Countries*, Oxford Academic, http://dx.doi.org/10.1162/qjec.2007.122.4.1351. [44]

BMAS (2020), *Fachkräfte sichern: weiter bilden und Gleichstellung fördern" (Sozialpartnerrichtlinie)*, https://www.initiative-fachkraefte-sichern.de/hauptnavigation/antragstellung/aufbau-von-personalentwicklungsstrukturen.html. [37]

BMAS (2020), *Qualifizierungschancengesetz*, https://www.bmas.de/DE/Service/Gesetze/qualifizierungschancengesetz.html. [17]

BMAS (2020), *UnternehmensWert: Mensch program*, https://www.unternehmens-wert-mensch.de/startseite.html. [36]

BMWi (2019), *SMEs Digital - Strategies for the digital transformation*, Federal Ministry for Economic Affairs and Energy (BMWi). [60]

Cedefop (2020), *Cedefop database on financing adult learning*, https://www.cedefop.europa.eu/en/publications-and-resources/tools/financing-adult-learning-db/search/impulse-qualification-network. [54]

Cedefop (2018), *Netherlands: public-private partnerships will promote innovation in VET*, https://www.cedefop.europa.eu/en/news-and-press/news/netherlands-public-private-partnerships-will-promote-innovation-vet. [64]

Cedefop (2015), *Who trains in small and medium-sized enterprises: Characteristics, needs and ways of support*, Cedefop. [27]

Cedefop (2012), *Payback clauses in Europe: supporting company investment in training*, European Union. [26]

Cedefop (2009), *Using tax incentives to promote education and training*, European Union. [25]

Enterprise Ireland (2020), *Management Advice*, https://www.enterprise-ireland.com/en/Management/Access-Strategic-Advice-and-Expertise/. [49]

European Commission (2020), *Skills for SMEs - Cybersecurity, Internet of Things and Big Data for Small and Medium-Sized Enterprises*, European Union. [7]

European Commission (2020), *Study on mapping opportunities and challenges for micro and small enterprises in offering their employees up- or re- skilling opportunities,*. [24]

European Commission (2019), *Skills for Smart Industrial Specialisation and Digital Transformation*, European Union. [23]

European Commission (2018), *Skills audits: tools to identify talent*, European Union. [34]

European Digital SME Alliance (2020), , https://www.digitalsme.eu/digital-skills-resources/. [41]

FFG (2020), *COMET – Competence Centers for Excellent Technologies*, https://www.ffg.at/en/comet/programme. [61]

Gov.UK (2020), *Small business support schemes: Small Business Leadership Programme and Peer Networks*, https://www.gov.uk/guidance/small-business-support-schemes-small-business-leadership-programme-and-peer-networks#peer-networks. [50]

Indecon (2019), *Evaluation of Skillnet Ireland in 2018*. [48]

InnovaSouth (2020), , https://www.innovasouthproject.eu/methodology/. [38]

Irish Department of Education and Skills (2020), *Regional Skills Fora - Annual Report 2019*. [31]

Katapult (2020), , https://wearekatapult.eu/. [65]

Kreiling, L. and C. Paunov (2021), *Knowledge co-creation in the 21st century: A cross-country experience-based policy report*, OECD Science, Technology and Industry Policy Paper 115, https://doi.org/10.1787/c067606f-en. [58]

Larosse, J. (2017), *Analysis of national initiatives on digitising European Industry: Denmark*. [62]

MADE Digital (2020), , https://www.made.dk/digital/. [63]

Marchese, M. et al. (2019), "Enhancing SME productivity: Policy highlights on the role of managerial skills, workforce skills and business linkages", *OECD SME and Entrepreneurship Papers*, No. 16, OECD Publishing, Paris, https://dx.doi.org/10.1787/825bd8a8-en. [46]

Mason, C. and R. Brown (2014), "Entrepreneurial ecosystems and growth-oriented entrepreneurship". [66]

Ministère du Travail, de l'Emploi et de l'Insertion (2014), *Gestion prévisionnelle de l'emploi et des compétences (GPEC)*, https://travail-emploi.gouv.fr/emploi/accompagnement-des-mutations-economiques/appui-aux-mutations-economiques/article/gestion-previsionnelle-de-l-emploi-et-des-competences-gpec. [33]

MKB!DEE (2020), *MKB!DEE*, https://mkbideenetwerk.nl/. [22]

OECD (2021), *Career Guidance for Adults in a Changing World of Work*, Getting Skills Right, OECD Publishing, Paris, https://dx.doi.org/10.1787/9a94bfad-en. [12]

OECD (2021), *Continuing Education and Training in Germany*, Getting Skills Right, OECD Publishing, Paris, https://dx.doi.org/10.1787/1f552468-en. [18]

OECD (2021), *The Digital Transformation of SMEs*, OECD Studies on SMEs and Entrepreneurship, OECD Publishing, Paris, https://dx.doi.org/10.1787/bdb9256a-en. [8]

OECD (2020), *An OECD Strategy for SMEs: Synthesis analysis on SMEs and skills*, Centre for Entrepreneurship, SMEs, Regions and Cities (CFE), https://one.oecd.org/document/CFE/SME(2020)8/ANN1/en/pdf. [6]

OECD (2020), *Continuous Learning in Working Life in Finland*, Getting Skills Right, OECD Publishing Paris, https://doi.org/10.1787/2ffcffe6-en. [20]

OECD (2020), *Digital business diagnostic tools for SMEs and entrepreneurship: A review of international policy experiences*, OECD Publishing, Paris, https://doi.org/10.1787/516bdf9c-en. [40]

OECD (2020), *Enhancing Training Opportunities in SMEs in Korea*, Getting Skills Right, OECD Publishing, Paris, https://doi.org/10.1787/7aa1c1db-en. [19]

OECD (2020), "Exploring policy options on teleworking: Steering local economic and employment development in the time of remote work", *OECD Local Economic and Employment Development (LEED) Papers*, No. 2020/10, OECD Publishing, Paris, https://dx.doi.org/10.1787/5738b561-en. [42]

OECD (2020), *Increasing Adult Learning Participation: Learning from Successful Reforms*, Getting Skills Right, OECD Publishing, Paris, https://dx.doi.org/10.1787/cf5d9c21-en. [9]

OECD (2020), *Workforce Innovation to Foster Positive Learning Environments in Canada*, Getting Skills Right, OECD Publishing, Paris, https://dx.doi.org/10.1787/a92cf94d-en. [15]

OECD (2019), *Getting Skills Right: Engaging Low-skilled Adults in Learning*, OECD, Paris, https://www.oecd.org/els/emp/engaging-low-skilled-adults-2019.pdf. [21]

OECD (2019), *Getting Skills Right: Future-Ready Adult Learning Systems*, Getting Skills Right, OECD Publishing, Paris, https://dx.doi.org/10.1787/9789264311756-en. [2]

OECD (2019), *Individual Learning Accounts: Panacea or Pandora's Box?*, OECD Publishing, Paris, https://doi.org/10.1787/203b21a8-en. [11]

OECD (2019), *OECD SME and Entrepreneurship Outlook 2019*, OECD Publishing, Paris, http://dx.doi.org/10.1787/34907e9c-en. [1]

OECD (2019), *University-Industry Collaboration: New Evidence and Policy Option*, OECD Publishing, Paris, https://doi.org/10.1787/e9c1e648-en. [57]

OECD (2018), *Getting Skills Right: Brazil*, OECD Publishing, Paris, https://doi.org/10.1787/9789264309838-en. [35]

OECD (2018), *Good Jobs for All in a Changing World of Work: The OECD Jobs Strategy*, OECD Publishing, Paris, http://dx.doi.org/10.1787/9789264308817-en. [5]

OECD (2018), "HEInnovate framework and good practice statements", in *Supporting Entrepreneurship and Innovation in Higher Education in The Netherlands*, OECD Publishing, Paris, https://dx.doi.org/10.1787/9789264292048-13-en. [14]

OECD (2017), *Financial Incentives for Steering Education and Training*, Getting Skills Right, OECD Publishing, Paris, https://doi.org/10.1787/9789264272415-en. [3]

OECD (2017), *Key issues for digital transformation in the G20*. [47]

OECD (2016), *Getting Skills Right: Assessing and Anticipating Skill Needs*, OECD Publishing, https://doi.org/10.1787/9789264252073-en. [30]

OECD (2013), *Skills Development and Training in SMEs*, OECD Skills Studies, OECD Publishing, Paris, https://dx.doi.org/10.1787/9789264169425-en. [13]

OECD/European Union (2019), *Supporting Entrepreneurship and Innovation in Higher Education in Italy*, OECD Skills Studies, OECD Publishing, Paris, https://dx.doi.org/10.1787/43e88f48-en. [59]

OECD/ILO (2017), *Engaging Employers in Apprenticeship*, OECD Publishing, https://doi.org/10.1787/9789264266681-en. [10]

Ramboll (2018), *Kickstart Digitalisering Utvärdering - Evaluation of Kickstart Digitalisering*, Ramboll Management Consulting. [52]

Regional Skills Forum (2020), *Skills for Growth*, https://www.regionalskills.ie/skills-for-growth/. [32]

Sgarzi, M. (2019), *Upskilling pathways in France*, CEREQ. [29]

Skillnet Ireland (2020), , https://www.skillnetireland.ie/. [56]

Stone, I. (2012), *Upgrading workforce skills in small business: International review of policy and experience*, OECD, LEED, DBA. [4]

Stone, I. (2010), *Encouraging small firms to invest in training: learning from overseas*, UK Commission for Employment and Skills, http://www.ukces.org.uk/our-work/research-and-policy/praxis/. [16]

Tillväxtverket (2020), *Kickstart Digitalisering: Method to: inspire and increase the understanding and ability of industrial SMEs to implement digital solutions*, Tillväxtverket. [53]

Workplace Innovation Europe (2020), , https://workplaceinnovation.eu/. [39]

Notes

[1] For instance, the same ranking can be retrieved in the United Kingdom across all three waves of the Continuing Vocational Training Survey (2005, 2010, 2015), but only in the 2015 wave for Ireland.

[2] According to the a recent report of the European Commission, high-tech skills encompass the skills needs related to digital technologies (e-skills) and a group of six advanced technologies (ATs) including: micro and nano-electronics, nanotechnology, industrial biotechnology, advanced materials, photonics, and advanced manufacturing technologies, artificial intelligence and security and connectivity. The concept of T-shaped skills has emerged, referring to a combination of both general skills across multiple domains, and specialised skills within (at least) one domain. It refers mainly to programmes, projects and curricula that combine high-tech skills with specific complementary skills, namely: technical skills in adjacent domains; skills related to quality, risk and safety; management, entrepreneurial and leadership skills; communication; innovation; emotional intelligence skills and the ability to consider ethical implications (European Commission, 2019[23]).

[3] Workplace innovation is a type of workforce innovation: it is the testing, sharing and implementation of new approaches to work organisation, management practices and job design that leads to better use of workers' skills and more learning in the workplace (OECD, 2020[15]). The term "high performance work practices" refers to a set of human resources practices that include aspects of work organisation and job design such as teamwork, autonomy, task discretion, mentoring, job rotation, and applying new learning. They also include management practices such as employee participation, incentive pay, training practices and flexibility in working hours. Even though definitions vary, they are generally associated with greater skills use and informal learning, employee participation and discretionary effort at all levels of the organisation (OECD, 2020[15]).

[4] Ecosystems are defined as "a set of interconnected entrepreneurial actors (both potential and existing), entrepreneurial organisations (e.g. firms, venture capitalists, business angels, banks), institutions (universities, public sector agencies, financial bodies) and entrepreneurial processes (e.g. the business birth rate, numbers of high growth firms, levels of blockbuster entrepreneurship, number of serial entrepreneurs, degree of sell-out mentality within firms and levels of entrepreneurial ambition) which formally and informally coalesce to connect, mediate and govern the performance within the local entrepreneurial environment" (Mason and Brown, 2014[66]).

www.ingramcontent.com/pod-product-compliance
Lightning Source LLC
Chambersburg PA
CBHW062029210326
41519CB00060B/7367

* 9 7 8 9 2 6 4 8 9 3 5 5 9 *